JESUS WANTS
TO SAVE CHRISTIANS

JESUS WANTS TO SAVE CHRISTIANS

Learning to Read a Dangerous Book

ROB BELL
DON GOLDEN

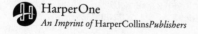
HarperOne
An Imprint of HarperCollins*Publishers*

HarperOne

JESUS WANTS TO SAVE CHRISTIANS: *Learning to Read a Dangerous Book*. Copyright © 2008 by Rob Bell and Don Golden. All rights reserved. Printed in the United States of America. No part of this book may be used or reproduced in any manner whatsoever without written permission except in the case of brief quotations embodied in critical articles and reviews. For information address HarperCollins Publishers, 10 East 53rd Street, New York, NY 10022.

HarperCollins books may be purchased for educational, business, or sales promotional use. For information please write: Special Markets Department, HarperCollins Publishers, 10 East 53rd Street, New York, NY 10022.

HarperCollins website: http://www.harpercollins.com

HarperCollins®, 📖®, and HarperOne™ are trademarks of HarperCollins Publishers

FIRST PUBLISHED BY ZONDERVAN IN 2008
FIRST HARPERCOLLINS EDITION PUBLISHED IN 2012

Library of Congress Cataloging-in-Publication Data

Bell, Rob.
Jesus wants to save Christians: learning to read a dangerous book /
Rob Bell, Don Golden. — 1st HarperCollins pbk. ed.
p. cm.
Includes bibliographical references.
ISBN 978-0-06-212582-8
1. Bible—Criticism, interpretation, etc. 2. Bible—Paraphrases, English.
I. Golden, Don. II. Title.
BS511.3.B46 2012
230—dc23   2012010235

12 13 14 15 16 RRD(H) 10 9 8 7 6 5 4 3 2 1

CONTENTS

PREFACE

Part One

I remember the exact moment when I knew that Don and I had a book on our hands.

We were eating our usual once a week burrito discussing our usual topics—revolution, Jesus, our favorite British bands—you know, average sorts of things friends talk about, when Don asked me how King Solomon had built his temple.

How Solomon built his temple? What an odd question.

I had read that story about Solomon building a temple for God in the Old Testament Book of Kings, but I had no recollection of how he built it.

The answer? Don pointed out that Solomon built the temple using slave labor.

Hearing that for me was like a bomb going off.

Slaves? I'd never noticed that. The implications were stunning.

The earlier parts of the Bible, the ones about empires and power and liberation from slavery, suddenly took on new meaning. The prophets, and then Jesus, began to mean something different. And then the church, and the New Testament letters connecting Jesus and the Exodus began to make sense in ways I'd never considered.

And then Don kept going. He made connections between Solomon's slaves and Egypt and Sinai and Jerusalem and Babylon and America and Iraq and politics and economics and churches and media . . . it was overwhelming. As we discussed more and more over the next weeks and months, rereading the stories of Jesus through this lens, I often felt like I was reading the Bible for the first time.

And the story that it was telling blew me away.

Reading the Bible through this new lens was so much more current and volatile and true and interesting and dangerous and subversive and hopeful and big than how I'd read it before.

Yes, I kept telling Don, there is a book here.

So that's my hope for you with this book: I hope you have a series of those "bomb going off" kind of moments as you read this book. I hope you see in our reading and interpreting of this ancient book, the Bible, a new way of seeing our world. I hope you see that there is a common humanity we share with everybody alive today, and everybody who has come before us. I hope you see in the way the writers of the Bible critique their own use and abuse of power and blessing a way for us to think about our power and blessing.

And then, most of all, I hope you see Jesus's invitation to be a force for good in the world, to wake up to our calling, to be saved in all of the ways that matter most.

—*Rob Bell*
  November 2011

Part Two

On Christmas Eve 1968 the first humans orbited the moon. Highly trained Apollo 8 astronauts were ready for every eventuality—except one. The first photo of Earth from outer space unexpectedly shook the imagination of the world. This one shot of our fragile blue orb alone in the infinitude of space revealed our majesty and our vulnerability. By going to the moon we discovered ourselves.

We hope a similar change in perspective happens when you read this book.

Jesus Wants to Save Christians offers a different perspective on the Bible and on how we see ourselves at the beginning of the twenty-first century.

Since we mostly retell the Bible's story through a new lens, the book's message hasn't changed since it was first released. But there are new challenges and new questions in a world that seems somehow scarier today than it did during the fires of President Bush's wars.

For some, President Bush was an easy parallel to Solomon and Pharaoh. We argued that power exists for the cause of the poor and that America will be measured by the voices we fail to hear. Since the book was first published in 2008, some major punctuation points have been added: Arab Spring—what Bush tried with bombs, social media masses achieved with their thumbs. The

Hummer dealership on 28th Street in Grand Rapids closed. In many ways, the world seems changed.

But the Bible still has a lot to say about empires. The Bible is always asking about the prospects of the poor. The vulnerability index is the measure that matters most in God's economy. Read seriously, the Bible confronts the reader with the God of the oppressed.

We want you to discover the Bible as its own best commentary. We offer you a way to read the Bible that doesn't require a library or a preacher or a politician or an academic to interpret for you. Once *justice* is seen as the thread woven into the fabric of biblical history, the whole Bible becomes much clearer. Justice is the issue when God redeems Israel from Pharaoh. Justice is at the heart of the Sinai law and justice is what Israel must show the world as a kingdom of priests. Justice is the measure the Jews failed to meet in their days of power and empire in Jerusalem. It was justice the prophets proclaimed as the way of return during the exile of the Jews in Babylon and it was justice that Jesus incarnated.

Some readers have told me that after reading the book it was still not clear what they should do with this new perspective on the Bible. Mostly, I think that is part of the adventure of discovery that we hope God leads you on. For me, though, I can say that when I look around and see what God is doing in the world, I tend to see, first, the people and ministries who incarnate this Exodus ethic. I'm thinking of friends like David and Marianne and Sam and Dr. Pieter.

David is a forty-two-year-old man in northern Kenya who does whatever it takes to help the Turkana suffering without food and water. David embodies the cry of the oppressed that God uses to kick-start redemptive history. David is pouring his life out to save Turkana.

Marianne is a recent Bible college graduate who travels the world photographing development professionals, capturing their amazing work in images that motivate people to action. Marianne's eye for the human story makes the plight and the possibilities of the poor live in high definition. Marianne helps us hear the cry of the oppressed.

Sam is a teacher from rural Pennsylvania who moved to Baltimore's inner city with a tribe of others just like him. Sam and co., with all their middle-American gifts, have set out to love on Baltimore neighborhoods most people abandoned a generation ago. Sam is the man who hears what God hears and joins what God is doing.

Dr. Pieter left his home in Johannesburg to discover the causes of child mortality in Mozambique. Dr. Pieter and his alternative community of life-giving workers have literally moved the needle on child mortality in southern Mozambique.

A doctor battles the mass murdering, malarial mosquito. A teacher spends his education on embattled Baltimore public schools. A poor Turkana man tries to save his ancient people from extinction. A young suburbanite with a camera takes aim at American indifference. Each one and countless others following Jesus out of the exile of irrelevance into what God is doing in history—redeeming people and using them to save others.

We hope this paperback edition of *Jesus Wants to Save Christians* helps you encounter the Bible in a new way. Like a trip to the moon, may you see the big picture and may the God of the oppressed lead you through these disorienting days of teetering empire.

—*Don Golden*
  November 2011

JESUS WANTS
TO SAVE CHRISTIANS

INTRODUCTION
TO THE INTRODUCTION

This is a book about a book.

The structure follows the narrative of the Bible, which means that there is a progression here, each chapter building on the one before it. If you skip ahead, it's not going to make much sense.

Before we begin, a disclaimer and a shout-out or two.

First, the disclaimer.

In the scriptures, ultimate truths about the universe are revealed through the stories of particular people living in particular places. As this book explores, the nation of Egypt and the Jewish people feature prominently in the biblical narrative. When we write of Egypt *then*, we are not writing about Egypt *today*. When we mention the Jews *then*, we are not speaking of our Jewish friends and neighbors *today*. We realize that some of these words, such as *Egypt* and *the Jews*, have power to evoke feelings and thoughts and attitudes about the very pain and division in our world that this book addresses. We join you in this tension, believing that the story is ultimately about healing, hope, and reconciliation.

And now, a shout-out. This is a book of theology. The word *theology* comes from two Greek words: *theo*, which means "God," and *logos*, which means "word."

Theology, a word about God.

Anybody can do theology.[1]

This book is our attempt to articulate a specific theology, a particular way to read the Bible, referred to by some as a New Exodus perspective. One New Exodus scholar is a British theologian named Tom Holland, who has done pioneering work in this approach.[2] We are grateful to him for his groundbreaking take on the story of Jesus. He has liberated profound truths about what it means to be human, and we celebrate that with him.

One more shout-out, which is actually a massive shout-out. We are part of a church, a community of people learning to live the way of Jesus together. For their love and support and critique and questions and example and insight and hope, we are deeply grateful.

You know who you are.

Grace and peace to you.

And thanks.

Now, on to "Air Puffers and Rubber Gloves."

AIR PUFFERS AND RUBBER GLOVES

The first family was dysfunctional.

At least, that's the picture painted by the storyteller in the book of Genesis.

The first son, Cain, was angry with the other first son, Abel, because "the LORD looked with favor on Abel and his offering, but on Cain and his offering he did not look with favor."[1]

Cain said to his brother, "Let's go out to the field." And when they went, Cain killed Abel.

According to the story, Cain "worked the soil" while Abel "kept flocks." One was a farmer, the other was a shepherd.

A farmer is settled.

A farmer has chosen a piece of land and settled there because he's decided that this land can best support his crops. He has a strong sense of boundaries—this land, the land that he lives on and farms, is his land.

A shepherd is nomadic.

A shepherd goes wherever there is food for his flock. A shepherd wanders from place to place. A shepherd doesn't have a strong sense of boundaries, because he sees all land as a possible spot for him to stop and feed his flock.

It wouldn't take long for the shepherd and his flock to cross onto the property of the farmer. And that would raise the question, Whose land is it, anyway?

This question would have many dimensions—economic, political, religious, social—let alone the personal aspects of ownership and property and progress and wealth. The story of these two first sons is actually a story about progress, innovation, and the inevitable forward movement of human civilization.[2]

This Genesis account reflects the transition that was occurring in the time and place in which this story was first told. A seismic shift was occurring as human society transitioned from a pastoral, nomadic orientation to an agricultural one. This was a huge change that did not come without a lot of strife.

And, occasionally, murder.

As a result of the murder, the text says, "Cain went out from the Lord's presence and lived in the land of Nod, east of Eden."[3]

East of Eden.

There is a place called Eden, a paradise, a state of being in which everything is in its right place. A realm where the favor and peace of God rest on everything.

And Cain is not there. He's east of there.

And he's not only east of Eden, but in chapter 4 of the book of Genesis, the text says that he was "building a city."[4]

It's not just that he's east of where he was created to live, but he's actually settling there, building a city, putting down roots. The land of his wandering has become the location of his home. And then several chapters later, the Bible says that the whole world had one language and a common speech "as people moved eastward."[5]

The writer, or writers, of Genesis keeps returning to this eastward metaphor,[6] insisting that something has gone terribly wrong with humanity, and that from the very beginning humans are moving in the wrong direction.[7]

God asks Adam, "Where are you?"[8]

And the answer is, of course, "East."

East of where he's supposed to be. East of how things are meant to be.

There is a new invention at the airport. Before we board our plane, we have to go through security. Many of us have had the joy of standing there in our socks, with our belt off, desperately searching our pockets for anything metal that could set off the detector and cause us to be subjected to the wand, a handheld device that is passed over the body, beeping when it detects anything made of metal. The wand is difficult enough, but when the person using it is wearing rubber gloves … it just doesn't help the experience, does it?

One of us, after being selected for a random security check, was asked with a straight face by a Transportation Safety Administration official, "Would you like me to give you a full-body pat down here? Or we could step into a private room off to the side, if you'd find that preferable."

But enough of our traumatic airport flashbacks. There's a new invention at the security checkpoint called the air puffer. It's only for people who have been "randomly" selected for extra security measures. The air puffer is about the size of a phone booth. We step into it, it makes a low buzzing sound, and then it shoots bursts of air all over our body. A green light then comes on, the glass doors in front open, and we're free to exit. We are given no instructions and receive no explanation as to why exactly being shot with little bursts of air all over one's body makes the world a safer place. Apparently, it has something to do with detecting the presence of explosive substances.

What is most frightening about the air puffer is not the unexpected puffs of air. What is most frightening is that we do it. Thousands of us each day step in, feel the breeze, wait for the light, exit, and then set off in search of our belt and shoes. Because if we were to protest, we would immediately be escorted into "a private room to the side" for who knows what.

And besides, we have to catch our plane.

Now, as we leave the air puffer, collect our belongings, and make our way toward the gate our plane is departing from, the first thing we hear is a television. There are many of them all over the terminal. They are set to the same channel, a news show that is custom-made for airports. The length of the segment before it repeats is about the average length of time a person sits waiting for their plane. This news channel gives up-to-date pictures and reports on news from around the world, including the latest word from the government on just how safe or unsafe it is to travel.

Which takes us back to the air puffer. On the side of the air puffer is a logo. A large logo of a very well-known, very large American company that has made hundreds of millions of dollars over the years selling convenient, time-saving devices for every aspect of our lives. And now, in addition to toasters and irons and refrigerators, they manufacture and sell air puffers.

Keeping us safe is very, very profitable.

Which takes us back to the televisions, where a reporter is showing us pictures of a brand-new plane the American military has just unveiled that cost fifty billion dollars to create. This plane can do what no other plane can do—it can hover like a helicopter and then fly like a jet—and this particular television network has been granted the privilege of taking the first civilian flight aboard this wonder of technology and innovation.[9]

Which takes us back to something that's next to the air puffer: a fully equipped security checkpoint that is not in use and has been roped off. It is brand-new and next to it is a sign describing the advanced features of this new machine and how this is the security checkpoint of the future. It even has little walls with detectors in them that you walk between so you don't have to take off your shoes.

Being safe is getting more convenient by the moment.

Which takes us back to the television. The reporter is now talking about a recent debate among government leaders concerning funding for homeland security. Various members are arguing for and against certain sums for increased security measures, and somewhere in the course of the broadcast it is stated that the war America is fighting is on its way to costing a trillion dollars. For purposes of the debate, a distinction is being made between the cost of the war *over there* and the cost of ensuring our safety *here*. The nearly trillion dollars is for the effort *over there*, and there's another budget for our security *here*, and it is an equally mind-blowing amount of money. When we hear it, we think, "That's a lot of air puffers and rubber gloves."

Which takes us back to the air puffer. The air puffer that we paid for with our tax dollars. To keep us safe, with our tax dollars, from the people we're fighting. To hear about every day on the news we're paying for with our consumption of the products advertised during the commercial breaks from the news—the news that tells us how unsafe the world is.

Which takes us back to the television, to a report they are now doing about how gas prices are going to go up again and global supplies of oil simply aren't what they used to be.

We hear this news as we walk by an advertisement on the wall for a large American-made automobile. It seats seven people and has a television. This vehicle does not get very many miles to the gallon.

One can't help but wonder, Is there an enemy of America, hiding somewhere in a cave, laughing? Already plotting some other way to harm us that will have nothing to do with airplanes?

Or are they plotting nothing?

Because they realize that whatever they might do next, it would be nowhere as destructive as what we're already doing to ourselves.[10]

We are east of Eden.

Something is not right.

The Germans have a word for this. They call it *Ursprache* (oor´shprah-kah). *Ursprache* is the primal, original language of the human family.[11] It's the language of paradise that still echoes in the deepest recesses of our consciousness, telling us that things are out of whack deep in our bones, deep in the soul of humanity. Something about how we relate to one another has been lost. Something is not right with the world.

Back to the television in the airport. On the news are sound bites from a speech by the president of the United States. He's on the deck of an aircraft carrier, proclaiming victory in a recent military effort. Not only was the mission accomplished, according to the leader of the world's only superpower, but American forces are now occupying this Middle Eastern country until peace can be fully realized within its borders.

This puts a Christian in an awkward place.

Because Jesus was a Middle Eastern man who lived in an occupied country and was killed by the superpower of his day.

The Roman Empire, which put Jesus on an execution stake, insisted that it was bringing peace to the world through its massive military might, and anybody who didn't see it this way just might be put on a cross. Emperor Caesar, who ruled the Roman Empire, was considered the "Son of God," the "Prince of Peace," and one of his propaganda slogans was "peace through victory."[12]

The insistence of the first Christians was that through this resurrected Jesus Christ, God has made peace with the world. Not through weapons of war but through a naked, bleeding man hanging dead on an execution stake. A Roman execution stake. Another of Caesar's favorite propaganda slogans was "Caesar is Lord." The first Christians often said "Jesus is Lord." For them, Jesus was another way, a better way, a way that made the world better through sacrificial love, not coercive violence.[13]

So when the commander in chief of the most powerful armed forces humanity has ever seen quotes the prophet Isaiah from the Bible in celebration of military victory,[14] we must ask, Is this what Isaiah had in mind?

A Christian should get very nervous when the flag and the Bible start holding hands. This is not a romance we want to encourage.

And the *Ursprache* continues to echo within each one of us, telling us that things aren't right, that we're up against something very old,
and very deep,

and very wide,
and very, very powerful.

For a growing number of people in our world, it appears
that many Christians support some of the very things
Jesus came to set people free from.

It's written in Genesis that when Cain killed Abel, God
said to Cain, "Your brother's blood cries out to me from
the ground."[15]

God can hear Abel's blood?

Blood that cries out?

To understand this cry, the noise that it makes across
human history, and its importance to the times we live in,
we have to go back to the first book of the Bible, the
book of Exodus.

CHAPTER ONE

THE CRY OF THE OPPRESSED

The first book of the Bible … Exodus?

Well, yes, and, of course, no.

No, because the first book of the Bible is Genesis. At least when a person picks it up and starts reading from the "in the beginning God created" part.

And yes, because many scholars see Exodus, the second book of the Bible, as the book in which the central story of redemption begins—liberation from Egypt.[1]

Egypt, the superpower of its day, was ruled by Pharaoh, who responded to the threat of the growing number of Israelites in his country by forcing them into slavery. They had to work every day without a break, making bricks, building storehouses for Pharaoh.[2]

Egypt is an empire,
built on the backs of Israelite slave labor,
brick by
brick by
brick.

But right away in the book of Exodus, there is a
disruption. Things change. And the change begins with
God saying:

"I have indeed seen the misery of my people ..."
"I have heard them crying out ..."
"I have come down to rescue them ..."
"I have seen the way the Egyptians are oppressing
them ..."[3]

A God who sees and hears. A God who hears the cry. The
Hebrew word used here for cry is *sa'aq,* and we find it all
throughout the Bible. *Sa'aq* is the expression of pain, the
ouch, the sound we utter when we are wounded.[4]

But *sa'aq,* is also a question, a question that arises out of
the pain of the wound. Where is justice? Did anybody see
that? Who will come to my rescue? Did anybody hear
that? Or am I alone here?

Sa'aq is what Abel's blood does from the ground after
he's killed by his brother.

The Israelites are oppressed, they're in misery, they're
suffering—and when they cry out, God hears.

This is a God who always hears the cry.

This is central to who God is: God *always* hears the cry of the oppressed.

The cry inaugurates history. It kicks things in gear. It shakes things up and gets them moving. The cry is the catalyst, the cause, the reason that a new story unfolds.

But God in this story doesn't just hear the cry. God does something about it. The exodus is how God responds to the cry.

Think about your life. What are the moments that have shaped you the most? If you were to pick just a couple, what would they be? Periods of transformation, times when your eyes were opened, decisions you made that affected the rest of your life.

How many of them came when you reached the end of your rope?

When everything fell apart?
When you were confronted with your powerlessness?
When you were ready to admit your life was unmanageable?
When there was nothing left to do but cry out?

For many people, it was their cry,
their desperation,
their acknowledgment of their oppression,
that was the beginning of their liberation.

When we're on top, when the system works for us, when we are capable of managing our lives, what is there for God to do?

But the cry—the cry inaugurates redemptive history. These slaves in Egypt cry out and God hears and something new happens. Things aren't how they were. Things change.

These slaves are rescued from the oppression of Egypt.

Egypt

In the Bible, Egypt is a place, a country, a nation where the story begins. But it's much, much more. To understand how central Egypt is to the flow of the biblical story, we have to go back to the introduction to the Bible, to the garden of Eden.

We're told Adam and Eve chose to go their own way, to explore outside of the boundaries given to them by their maker, and as a result, their relationship suffers. This story is immediately followed by the story of their son Cain killing their other son, Abel.

This is a rapid, dramatic progression from Adam and Eve to their sons. We've gone from eating fruit to murder in one generation. Things are falling apart very quickly.

Not only that, but right after the murder, a close descendant of Cain's, Lamech, laments that if "Cain is avenged seven times, then Lamech seventy-seven times."[5] The escalation of societal violence is so intense that a close relative of Cain's says things are eleven times worse than they were before. And then by chapter 6 of Genesis, just a few chapters after Cain and Abel, we find out that the whole world is headed for destruction except for one man and his family. And then by chapter 11, people have gotten together to build a tower that they are convinced will make them gods.

What started with two people and some fruit has escalated to murder among family members, to an entire civilization at odds with God.

The story is a tragic progression: the broken, toxic nature at the heart of a few humans has now spread to the whole world.

What started in a garden is now affecting the globe.

The word for this condition is *anti-kingdom*.[6]

There is God's kingdom—the peace, the *shalom*,[7] the good that God intends for all things. And then there is what happens when entire societies and systems and empires become opposed to God's desires for the world.

Imagine a slave girl living in Egypt asking her father why he's got a bandage on his arm. He tells her he was beaten by his master that day. She wants to know why. He explains to her that the quotas have recently been changed and he's now required to make the same amount of bricks as before, but he has to get his own straw.[8] He tells her that he's been falling behind in his brick production and that's why he was beaten. She then asks why his master couldn't just let it slide—why the beating? He explains that if the quotas aren't met, his master will be beaten by *his* master. And if *his* master doesn't make the quotas, he'll be beaten by his overseer, and so on up the chain of command, which goes all the way to Pharaoh. The father tries to make the daughter understand that yes, the beating came from one particular man, his master. But his master is part of a larger system, a complex web of power and violence and industry and technology that exploits people for its expansion and profit.

The bandage on the father's arm is from a wound inflicted by one man, and yet it's also from an entire system of injustice. This girl's family is facing an evil in the individual human heart that went unchecked until it gathered a head of steam and is now embedded in the very fabric of that culture.

That is anti-kingdom.

Egypt is an anti-kingdom.

Egypt is what happens when sin builds up a head of steam.

Egypt is what happens when sin becomes structured and embedded in society.

Egypt shows us how easily human nature bends toward using power to preserve privilege at the expense of the weak.

Imagine this girl asking her father more questions—questions not just about their life in Egypt but about their history: How did we get here in the first place? If we're Israelites, why aren't we living in Israel?

Imagine this young slave girl being told the Genesis story of how they became slaves. The escalation of violence that began with the first sons culminates in chapter 11 with the story of the Tower of Babel. And what are they building the Tower of Babel with?

Bricks.[9]

These slaves in Egypt, being forced to make bricks all day, would understand the Tower of Babel story. They would probably say, "We know what happens when people start building empires out of bricks."

Exodus is about a people, a tribe, a nation being rescued from slavery.

It's about liberation from occupation.

It's about the insurgent power of redemption from empire.

God sends a shepherd named Moses to lead them out of Egypt. Moses challenges Pharaoh, they go back and forth over who exactly this God is and why Pharaoh should even listen, and eventually the night comes when they gather up their things and leave Egypt. Three days later the Israelites cross a sea, an event that is later referred to as the baptism of Moses,[10] and on the shore they dance in celebration of their liberation.[11]

Which would make a nice ending to the story.

But it's not the end. It's actually a beginning. Their journey takes them to the foot of a mountain—a mountain called Sinai.

And what happens at Sinai is revolutionary,
not just for these former slaves,
and not just for the story of the Bible,
but for all of humanity.

Sinai

It's here, at Sinai, that God speaks.

God hasn't talked to a group of people since Eden. Things have been quiet, an eerie sort of silence. There have been exchanges with individuals—such as Abraham and Noah—but not with the masses.[12]

So when Moses tells the people at Sinai to "prepare yourselves" and then leads them out of the camp "to meet with God,"[13] this is about way more than a group of wilderness wanderers gathering for a message from the heavens. This is about humanity estranged from its maker. This is about the primal distance that exists between the divine and the human, the gap deep in the soul of humanity. Sinai is an answer to God's question to Adam, "Where are you?" This moment at Sinai is about the reversal of the consequences of Eden.

Sinai is the breaking of the silence.

God is near.

God is about to speak.

It's believed that this is the only faith tradition in human history that has as its central event a god speaking to a group of people all at one time.[14]

It has simply never happened in the history of the world.

And it happens in the wilderness, which has global implications. Because the Sinai event happened in the wilderness and not in the midst of a nation or city or province where someone could make ownership claims, it was for all the people of the world.[15]

Before God speaks directly to the people, God tells Moses to remind them of the exodus. "You yourselves have seen what I did to Egypt, and how I carried you on eagles' wings and brought you to myself."[16]

It's all grace.

It's all a gift.

Rescue, redemption, liberation—it's all received from God.

"Now if you obey me fully and keep my covenant ..."[17]

The word covenant is the Hebrew word *berit*. It's where we get the word testament, as in Old or New Testament. *Berit* carries the idea "to cut a deal."[18] It comes from an ancient Near Eastern practice relating to business, legal, and marriage agreements. God invites the people to make a covenant—a marriage of sorts. The divine and the human, coming together in a sacred wedding ceremony.

God continues, "Although the whole earth is mine, you will be for me a kingdom of priests and a holy nation."[19]

Priests?

A priest mediates the divine. To mediate is to come between. A priest comes between people and a god or gods. A priest shows you what his or her god is like.

When you go to a temple or shrine and you see the priest there—what they do, what they say about it, the rituals they perform—you get a sense for what their god cares about, who their god cares about.

So when God invites the people to be priests, it's an invitation to show the world who this God is and what this God is like.

Now there were hints of this invitation earlier, before they left Egypt. In Exodus 7, Moses was going to confront Pharaoh and command that he let the people go. The text reads, "Then the LORD said to Moses, 'See, I have made you like God to Pharaoh.'"[20]

Like God?

God is telling Moses that Pharaoh will see him as God, or at least "like God"?

And this is not Moses's idea; it's God's idea. What's going on here?

The answer leads us to a universal truth: God needs a body. God needs flesh and blood. God needs bones and skin so that Pharaoh will know just who this God is he's dealing with and how this God acts in the world. And not just so Pharaoh will know but so that all of humanity will know.

This is the God who liberates from oppression.

But God doesn't just invite them to be priests; he invites them to be a "holy nation."[21] The word nation takes us back to Genesis. Genesis is about the progression of sin, violence, and death—what started with one son killing the other quickly led to an entire civilization in opposition to God. And then Exodus begins with the Israelites[22] enslaved by a nation. Sin always gains a head of steam when it goes unchecked. And that always leads to institutions and cultures and structures that are anti-kingdom. This leads to dehumanizing places, like Egypt had become, which these former slaves standing at the base of Sinai know all too well. And God's response is to form a different kind of nation, a "holy" one shaped not by greed, violence, and abusive power but by compassion, justice, and care for one's neighbor.

It's as if God says, "You've experienced Egypt; now I'm calling you to be the anti-Egypt." Up until now, God has been speaking to the people through Moses. But a point comes when God speaks directly to the people, beginning with the words, "I am the LORD your God, who brought you out of Egypt, out of the land of slavery."[23]

Of course.

The only way to understand this covenant relationship between God and the people is to understand what they've already been through together. Their relationship is rooted in an act of deliverance that God has performed on their behalf.

This is not an abstract God who floats above the blood and dirt and pain of the world. This is a God who is fundamentally defined by action on behalf of the oppressed.[24]

"I am the LORD ... who brought you out."

And then it's here, at Sinai, with the reminder of their liberation floating in the air, that God gives them the Ten Commandments.

Many people are familiar with the Ten Commandments, which are often portrayed as strict rules given by a fire-breathing God to keep people in line. But when they're seen in their original context, the commandments take on all sorts of new meanings.

Remember, these people have been living, up until very recently, as slaves. Slavery is a fundamentally inhumane condition. Being owned and treated as property robs people of the dignity and honor of being a human. This has deeply affected how these Israelites see themselves and the world around them. What God begins here at Sinai with the Ten Commandments is the long process of teaching them how to be human again. These commands are vital truths about what it means to live in authentic human community.

The first commandment instructs the people to "have no other gods."[25] Their humanity is directly connected to their ability to remember their liberation, which was a gift from God. If they forget God—the one, true God who freed them—they are at that very same moment forgetting their story. If they forget their story, they might forget what it was like to be slaves, and they might find themselves back in a new sort of slavery.

The second commandment builds on the first, prohibiting any "image in the form of anything."[26] In the ancient Near East, people conceptualized their many gods using images. They made statues and carvings and idols as physical representations of the divine beings they believed controlled their fate. A statue or carving gives shape and size and depth to the divine. An idol helped people understand just who their god was and what their god was like.

But this exodus God is different. This God is inviting these people to be priests, to show the world what this God is like through their lives. This God doesn't need images in the form of wood or stone or marble, because this God has people.

This God is looking for a body.

The command about idols and images leads to the third commandment, the prohibition not to "misuse the name of the LORD your God."[27] The Hebrew word for "misuse" here can also be translated "carry."[28] God has redeemed these former slaves and is now inviting them to be representatives in the world of this redemption and the God who made it happen. They are how the world will know who this God is. God's reputation is going to depend on them and how they "carry" God's name. The command is certainly about the words a person speaks. But at its heart it is far more about how Israel carries itself as those who carry the name of God. Will it act on behalf of the poor and oppressed? Because that is how this God acts.

The fourth commandment is to take a Sabbath, a day each week, and not do any work.[29] In Egypt, they worked every day without a break, being treated as objects to be exploited, not people.[30] The Sabbath is the command to take a day a week to remind themselves that they aren't in

Egypt anymore, that their value doesn't come from how many bricks they produce. Their significance comes from the God who rescued them, the God who loves them.

The Ten Commandments are a new way to be human, a new way to live and move in the world, in covenant with the God who hears the cry of the oppressed and liberates them.

Everything about the rest of the commandments speaks to this newfound liberation. God is inviting, God is looking, God is searching for a body, a group of people to be the body of God in the world.

Following the Ten Commandments are all sorts of laws and commands about how to live in this new way.[31] The Israelites are told not to charge interest. "If you take your neighbor's cloak as a pledge, return it by sunset, because that cloak is the only covering your neighbor has. What else can your neighbor sleep in? When he cries out to me, I will hear, for I am compassionate."[32]

Do you hear the echoes of Egypt in the command? If they begin to oppress on an individual basis, God says that when the oppressed cry out, "I will hear." The warning is sharp here: don't become another Pharaoh, because God acts *against* people like Pharaoh.

They're commanded, "Do not mistreat or oppress a foreigner, for you were foreigners in Egypt. Do not take advantage of a widow or an orphan.... Do not deny justice to your poor people."[33]

And God continually warns, "If you do [any of this] and they cry out to me, I will certainly hear their cry."[34]

It's as if God is saying, "The thing that has happened to you—go make it happen for others. The freedom from oppression that you are now experiencing—help others experience that same freedom. The grace that has been extended to you when you were at your lowest—extend it to others. In the same way that I heard your cry, go and hear the cry of others and act on their behalf."

God measures their faith by how they treat the widows, orphans, strangers—the weak—among them. God's desire is that they would bring exodus to the weak, in the same way that God brought them exodus in their weakness.

God's words to the people through Moses begin with "if you obey me fully."[35]

It's an invitation, an opportunity,
but it's a giant if, isn't it?

"If you obey me fully."

Which raises the question, Did they?
Were they true to the covenant?
How did they respond to the invitation?

We started with Egypt, we then went to Sinai, but to answer the "if" question, we now need to go to Jerusalem.

Jerusalem

Generations later, the descendants of these wandering slaves have settled into the land they were promised. Their great king David has secured their borders, the land and people are experiencing peace, and David's son Solomon comes to power. Solomon is brilliant and wise and wealthy, and Jerusalem, the capital of the kingdom, begins to gain a global reputation. A queen from the land of Sheba comes to visit Solomon.[36] She's from far away, from a different land, from a different kind of people, with a different religion. And she wants to know more about these people and their king and their God in Jerusalem.

Wasn't this what Sinai was all about?

God was looking for a body, a nation to show the world just who God is and what God is like. And now it's happening: foreigners from the corners of the earth are coming to ask questions and learn about just who this God is.

Sheba tests Solomon with hard questions,
she eats meals with him,
she watches him worship his God at the temple,
she gets a tour of his palace and all that he has built and acquired with his wealth,
and after surveying his kingdom,
she says, "Because of the LORD's eternal love for Israel, he has made you king to maintain justice and righteousness."[37]

Notice that she doesn't say he *is* maintaining justice and righteousness—only that there can be only one reason why he has received so much blessing from God.

And what does she mean by "justice and righteousness"?

Freedom, liberation from violence, protection from anything dehumanizing. She understands that God has given all of this wealth and power and influence so that Solomon would use it on behalf of those who are poor, weak, and suffering from injustice.

What impresses her most about this God of Solomon's is that this God is the God of the oppressed. This "pagan" queen from a foreign land understands what God is up to with these Jewish people living in Jerusalem.[38]

Sheba gets it.

So what did Solomon do with his wealth and power and influence? What kind of kingdom did he build? Did he maintain justice and righteousness with his vast resources?

Because it can go one of two ways in Jerusalem, can't it?

Solomon, like us, can use his power and wealth to do something about the cry of the oppressed, or he can turn a deaf ear.

The Bible tells the story: "Here is the account of the forced labor King Solomon conscripted to build the

LORD's temple, his own palace, the terraces, the wall of Jerusalem."³⁹

Another word for forced labor is, of course, slavery.

Solomon had slaves. Slaves who labored to build his temple, palace, and other buildings.

Wait.

The LORD's temple?

This is the same LORD who sets slaves free, correct?

The defining event of Solomon's ancestors was the exodus, right?

And now Solomon is building a temple for the God who sets slaves free ... using slaves?

This is a major moment in the Bible.

In just a few generations, the oppressed have become the oppressors.

The ancestors of people who once cried out because of their bondage are now causing others to cry out.

The descendants of people who once longed for freedom from Egypt are now building another Egypt.

Solomon has created an empire of indifference. He has forgotten the story of his ancestors. He hasn't remembered how Moses demanded that the people be set free, how they escaped from Pharaoh, how they were brought out on "eagles' wings."[40]

In a few generations these wandering former slaves who were newly rescued from an oppressive empire have become empire-builders themselves.

Solomon isn't maintaining justice; he's now perpetuating the very injustice his people once needed redemption from and, in the process, building a kingdom of comfort. He dines in his palace and strolls on terraces constructed by human suffering.

But it isn't just his comfort and indifference that stand out; it's what exactly he builds. In the section where we're told he was using slaves to build God's temple and his palace and the terraces, it also says that Solomon used these slaves to build "Hazor, Megiddo and Gezer."[41]

This is one of the many places in the Bible where it is easy to read through the lists of Hebrew names and miss what's going on right below the surface. So what are Hazor, Megiddo, and Gezer?

They're military bases.[42]

Megiddo is in a valley in the north of Israel. It's the valley where Africa, Europe, and Asia meet. It's a strategic location, to say the least. Megiddo is where we get the English word Armageddon.

Solomon is using his massive resources and wealth to build military bases to protect his … massive resources and wealth.

His empire-building leads him to place a high priority on preservation. Protecting and maintaining all that has been accumulated is taking more and more resources as attention is given to homeland security.

Not only that, but later in the text we're told that Solomon accumulated "fourteen hundred chariots and twelve thousand horses, which he kept in the chariot cities and also with him in Jerusalem."[43]

Horses? Chariots?

Pharaoh's soldiers rode on horses and in chariots as they chased the Hebrew slaves when they were escaping Egypt.

And the text goes on to say that Solomon imported them from Egypt!

Jerusalem is the new Egypt.

There's a new Pharaoh on the scene, and his name is Solomon, the son of David.

Not only is he accumulating horses and chariots, which were the tanks and fighter planes of his day, but the scriptures add that Solomon and his leaders "imported a chariot from Egypt for six hundred shekels of silver, and a horse for a hundred and fifty. They also exported them to all the kings of the Hittites and of the Arameans."[44]

Two words: import and export.

Solomon is buying horses and chariots, but he's also selling them. Solomon has become an arms dealer. He's now making money from violence. He's discovered that war is profitable.

Is that maintaining justice and righteousness?

Is that hearing the cry of the oppressed?

Is that looking out for the widow, the orphan, and the foreigner?

Shortly after this we read that Solomon "had seven hundred wives of royal birth and three hundred concubines, and his wives led him astray.... His wives turned his heart after other gods, and his heart was not fully devoted to the LORD his God."[45]

Seven hundred wives?

Three hundred concubines?

But the point for the storyteller is not the numbers; it's how his wives affected Solomon. They turned him away from God, and "his heart was not fully devoted."

This passage forms a significant contrast with what we learned earlier about the slaves and military bases. Those were systemic evils—Solomon creating an anti-kingdom—but now we learn about a different kind of failure, not a systemic one but the turning of an individual's heart.

Solomon breaks covenant with God.

This goes back to the first of the Ten Commandments, the one about having no other gods. Sinai was a marriage covenant between God and the people, a coming together of the divine and the human. And so the first commandment was that the people couldn't have other lovers. The relationship simply wouldn't work if they were unfaithful. Solomon's many wives and his infidelity to God are representative of the infidelity of all the people—they've turned from God. Tragically, Solomon's people had been warned that this could happen.

Moses said earlier that the king "must not acquire great numbers of horses for himself or make the people return to Egypt to get more of them, for the LORD has told you, 'You are not to go back that way again.' He must not take many wives, or his heart will be led astray. He must not accumulate large amounts of silver and gold."[46]

Did Solomon "acquire great numbers of horses"? Check.

Did he "take many wives"? Check.

Was his "heart led astray"? Check.

The text reads, "The weight of the gold that Solomon received yearly was 666 talents."[47] That's about twenty-five tons of gold.

Did he "accumulate large amounts of silver and gold"? Check.

And that number 666, the weight of the talents of gold? That's a very Jewish way of saying that something is evil, dark, wrong, and opposed to God.

Because it can go one of two ways in Jerusalem.

And with Solomon, the story takes a tragic turn.

Solomon goes "back that way again."
Jerusalem is the new Egypt,
Solomon is the new Pharaoh,
and Sinai has been forgotten.

This puts God in an awkward place.

Remember, God is looking for a body, flesh and blood to show the world a proper marriage of the divine and human.

What happens when your body looks nothing like you?

What happens when your people become the embodiment of everything you are against?

What happens when you're being given a bad name?

What happens when your people are unfaithful to the vow they made to you?

What happens when your people "go back that way again," the way you rescued them from?

Babylon

The Hebrew scriptures have a very simple and direct message:

God always hears the cry of the oppressed;

God cares about human suffering and the conditions that cause it.

God is searching for a body, a community of people to care for the things God cares about.

God gives power and blessing so that justice and righteousness will be upheld for those who are denied them.

This is what God is like. This is what God is about. This is who God is.

To forget this, to fail to hear the cry, to preserve prosperity at the expense of the powerless, is to miss what God has in mind.

At the height of their power, the Israelites misconstrued God's blessings as favoritism and entitlement. They became indifferent to God and to their priestly calling to bring liberation to others.

There's a word for this. A word for what happens when you still have the power and the wealth and the influence, and yet in some profound way you've blown it because you've forgotten why you were given it in the first place.

The word is exile.

Exile is when you forget your story.

Exile isn't just about location; exile is about the state of your soul.

Exile is when you fail to convert your blessings into blessings for others.

Exile is when you find yourself a stranger to the purposes of God.

And it's at this time that we meet the prophets, powerful voices who warned of the inevitable consequences of Israel's infidelity.[48]

The prophet Amos said, "Hear this word, people of Israel, the word the LORD has spoken against you—against the whole family I brought up out of Egypt: ... 'See the great unrest within her and the oppression among her people.

They do not know how to do right,' declares the LORD, 'who store up in their fortresses what they have plundered and looted.'"[49]

One of Amos's first charges is that some people are being neglected while others are stockpiling surplus. But then he says that because of this, Jerusalem is going to be destroyed: "'I will tear down the winter house along with the summer house; the houses adorned with ivory will be destroyed and the mansions will be demolished,' declares the LORD."[50]

The prophet Isaiah tells the people of Israel that when they pray, God says, "I will hide my eyes from you" because "your hands are full of blood."[51] God sees their military bases, chariots, and warhorses for what they are—unacceptable costs of empire.

And the prophets didn't stop with condemning the empire; they reserved their harshest critiques for the religion that animated it all. Isaiah declares that God hates "with all [his] being" their feasts and festivals and "evil assemblies."[52]

God calls their *church* services "evil assemblies"?[53]

God hates their religious gatherings?

When God is on a mission, what is God to do with a religion that legitimizes indifference and worship that inspires indulgence?

What is God to do when the time, money, and energy of his people are spent on ceremonies and institutions that neglect the needy?

Amos says, "Hear this word, you cows of Bashan on Mount Samaria, you women who oppress the poor and crush the needy."[54]

The cows of Bashan were known for how big and healthy and well fed they were. Amos compares the wealthy women of Israel to cows who graze gluttonously while others starve. God doesn't have a problem with eating and drinking and owning things. It's when those things come at the expense of others' having their basic needs met—that's when the passionate rants of the prophets really kick in.

And that word Amos uses: oppression? We first heard that word in Egypt.

Amos insists that God hates their worship: "Away with the noise of your songs! I will not listen to the music of your harps. But let justice roll on like a river, righteousness like a never-failing stream!... You who trample the needy and do away with the poor of the land,... buying the poor with silver and the needy for a pair of sandals."[55]

God is patient but also pragmatic. God has a plan. God cares about the suffering of the world and will not allow the indifference of his people to stand in the way of his plans to relieve that suffering.

Through Amos, God delivers the crushing blow: "Therefore you will be among the first to go into exile; your feasting and lounging will end."[56]

Amos predicts that the oppressors will be the first to be hauled away to a foreign land. How offensive would this be if you were a leader of Israel living in Jerusalem?

Amaziah the king, a descendant of Solomon, says in response to Amos's rants, "Get out!... Don't prophesy anymore ... because this is the king's sanctuary and the temple of the kingdom."[57]

Of course the king hates this message. How dare Amos bring these crushing words into the inner sanctum of power! Amos answers, "I was neither a prophet nor the disciple of a prophet, but I was a shepherd, and I also took care of sycamore-fig trees. But the LORD took me from tending the flock and said to me, 'Go, prophesy to my people Israel.' ... Therefore this is what the LORD says: 'Your wife will become a prostitute in the city, and your sons and daughters will fall by the sword.... And Israel will surely go into exile, away from their native land.'"[58]

The scene is overwhelming. A simple shepherd confronting the most powerful man in the nation with the message that the king is about to lose it all, the empire is over, it will not last, and when the king kicks him out, Amos says, "Oh, and by the way, your wife will become a prostitute and all your kids are going to be murdered."

Isaiah, Amos, Hosea—the prophets came to remind the people of Sinai, to bring the people back to the covenant they made with their God, to help them remember that God is looking for a body.

But Israel doesn't listen. It's written in 2 Chronicles that God sent them these prophets because God "had pity on his people and on his dwelling place."[59]

God wants to live among the people in the sacred union of the divine and human, but they aren't interested.

Chronicles continues, "But they mocked God's messengers, despised his words and scoffed at his prophets."[60]

Amos gets kicked out of the palace,
Jeremiah gets beaten up and put in stocks and thrown in a pit,
and the people don't change.

They don't remember Egypt.
They've forgotten Sinai.
They're too comfortable.

The system works for those with the power and influence to change the system. They can't hear the cry.

And so God suffers,[61] God is patient, God waits, but there comes a point when nothing more can be done.

Eventually "the king of the Babylonians ... killed their young men with the sword in the sanctuary, and spared neither young man nor young woman, the elderly or the aged.... He carried to Babylon all of the articles from the temple of God, both large and small, and the treasures of the Lord's temple and the treasures of the king and his officials. They set fire to God's temple and broke down the wall of Jerusalem; they burned all the palaces and destroyed everything of value there. He carried into exile to Babylon the remnant, who escaped from the sword, and they became servants to him and his successors until the kingdom of Persia came to power."[62]

Everything falls apart, the temple is destroyed, many are killed, and those who survive are carried off to a foreign land called Babylon.

And in Babylon, the survivors become "servants."

And what are servants who serve against their will?

Slaves.

The Israelites find themselves slaves in a foreign land.

Does this sound familiar?

Sounds a lot like Egypt, doesn't it?

CHAPTER TWO

GET DOWN YOUR HARPS

The descendants of Solomon find themselves enslaved in Babylon. They once had the palace and the temple and slaves and the thriving economy and the massive military.

And then, exile.

They used to be on top.
They used to have the power.
They used to rule.

But then, nothing.

They blew it.

They had wealth and influence and peace and blessing, but they lost it. They forgot their God, they neglected the widow and the orphan and the refugee, and everything fell apart.

In exile, however, they turned their pain into poetry.

"By the rivers of Babylon we sat and wept when we remembered [Jerusalem]. There on the poplars we hung our harps,... our tormentors demanded songs of joy.... How can we sing ... while in a foreign land?"[1]

They hung up their harps.

Harps were played in the temple area when worshipers came to Jerusalem to honor God and give offerings. The harp was an instrument of joy and celebration. People played the harp because they had reason to praise God.

The harp was a sound you heard when life was good.

But the Israelites are not in Jerusalem anymore; they're in Babylon.
Where they hang up their harps.
And they weep.
They cry out. In Babylon.

And what happens when people cry out? In Egypt, the cry kick-started redemption. In Egypt they cried out in their slavery, and God heard their cry and did something about it.

Because God always hears the cry of the oppressed.

When the system works for us, when we have the power and choice, when we're ruling from Jerusalem, when we have no needs to speak of, who needs to cry out?

Crying out reminds us of our dependence. Weeping leads us to reconnect with God.

Our tears are sacred. They water the ground around our feet so that new things can grow.[2]

It didn't take long for these exiles sitting by the side of the river in Babylon to connect their agony with the story of their ancestors who were slaves in Egypt. They knew *that* story. And now here they are, back in the same kind of oppressive situation.

If God freed our people once before, couldn't God do it again?

And so it's here,
in exile by the river,
amid the tears of despair,
that God's people begin to dream again.

Their repentance gives them hope to see a future beyond the bitterness of all they have lost.

Maybe those harps don't have to hang there forever.

Because it's when we're fully present in our pain,
when we're willing to sit in our tears,
that we're ready to imagine a different kind of tomorrow.

Take away the comforts of the kingdom, deprive people of the structures and institutions of empire, and they just might find the spine to envision a new tomorrow. Push them to the limits of suffering, and they just might become revolutionaries.

And that is what happened in exile.

Prophets rose up in the midst of all of the despair and hanging of harps and proclaimed not the end but the beginning of something new.

On the heels of colossal failure, the Jewish prophets imagined the greatest picture of hope and the future anybody's ever thought of anywhere.

Something new for them,
something new for all of humanity,
something new for all of creation.

The prophets of Israel came to the realization that what they needed was another exodus.
A new exodus.
A second exodus.

The prophet Isaiah said that in this new exodus they would "soar on wings like eagles."[3]

And of course "wings of eagles" is how God described the first exodus. And Isaiah says it's going to happen again: the Lord will reach out his hand a second time to reclaim the remnant of his people

from Assyria,
from Egypt,
from Cush,

from Elam,
from Babylonia,
from Hamath,
and from the islands of the sea.[4]

That long list of places?

Isaiah announces that God is going to bring these exiles home—and not just them but people from every corner of the earth. And God will do this, Isaiah says, because God wants people to "forget the former things." God is doing "a new thing."[5]

The former things? A new thing?

What these people in exile realize is that the former thing, the first exodus, simply wasn't big enough. The first exodus was just a hint of the redemption God has in mind for all of humanity.

Their ancestors had been set free only to find themselves in bondage again, first to their selfishness and arrogance, and then to the king of the Babylonians. Several generations later, they are slaves again. The prophets concluded that the next exodus would have to be bigger, wider, deeper, more enduring, more lasting than the first exodus.

Otherwise, how do they know *their* descendants won't repeat the same pattern? God will hear their cry, they'll be redeemed from exile, they'll return to Jerusalem, they'll build another empire, they'll forget their oppression as they oppress others, God will send them prophets to bring them back to their senses, they won't listen, and they'll find themselves watching another temple burn as they're led away to another foreign land.

The king of the Babylonians, the prophets concluded, wasn't the only problem any more than Pharaoh, the king of the Egyptians, was the only problem for their ancestors.

God had brought their ancestors out of the nation-state of Egypt, but there's a far deeper, more insidious kind of Egypt, the kind that warps the heart and causes people to hurt and abuse and exploit each other.

The real problem, the ultimate oppressor, is something that resides deep in every human heart. The real reason for their oppression is human slavery to violence, sin, and death.

There's an Egypt that we're all born into, and that's what we really need an exodus from.

So when Isaiah speaks of this new exodus, he doesn't just speak of liberation from a particular oppressive empire; he speaks of liberation from anything that oppresses anybody anywhere.

God, he insists, will "come and gather the people of all nations and languages, and they will come and see [God's] glory."[6]

By the rivers of Babylon, the prophets began to imagine
a God who is bigger than the narrow, tribal God of their
Jewish heritage.

But the prophets didn't stop there.

An exodus is a departure,
a leaving,
a movement.

It's motion,
energy,
action.

An exodus is something you do,
something you're caught up in,
somewhere you're going,
something you join because you don't want to stay where
you are.

The prophets called it "the way."

Isaiah says, "In the wilderness prepare the way ... make
straight in the desert a highway for our God."[7]

Wilderness? Desert? Once again, images from the first
exodus.

Isaiah continues, "All people will see it together."[8]

All people?

Apparently, anyone can join.
Everybody is welcome to come home.
People of "the way," headed home.

Isaiah says, "Leave Babylon, flee from the Babylonians!
Announce this with shouts of joy and proclaim it. Send it
out to the ends of the earth."[9]

"To the ends of the earth"?

This sounds like "all people."

What we see in the prophets' predictions again and again
is a movement from the particular to the universal. They
start by making promises to a specific ethnic group
about their leaving a specific geographic location, but
their expectations consistently expand until they're
talking about "all people."

Now, "the way" wasn't a new idea. Their ancestors had
spoken of how God provided a way for them out of
Egypt.[10] And *that* way had led them to a mountain called
Sinai.

As the Israelites continued to make the connection
between their torment in Babylon and their ancestors'
anguish in Egypt, they realized that they would have to
revisit what had happened at Sinai, because that's where
the heartache really began.

Remember the "if" at Sinai?[11]

God had promised that if they obeyed fully and were true and faithful, they would be a "kingdom of priests and a holy nation." God also made it clear that if they were unfaithful to their vows, if they turned from God and forgot their story and followed other gods, there would be consequences. Moses had laid out what those consequences would be, calling them "curses."[12]

But then, before Moses even returned from the mountain, these wandering former slaves had become impatient and began worshiping a golden calf, breaking the first agreement to have no other gods.[13]

So if Sinai was a marriage of sorts, it never really made it much past the ceremony. Israel continued turning from God until we hear of Solomon, who had seven hundred wives and three hundred concubines who led him to follow other gods.

As these exiles began to dream of a new exodus, then,
one that would be the way home,
one that would rescue them from every form of oppression,
they came to the realization that their exile was the consequence of their nation's infidelity.

Moses had said that if the Israelites obeyed God, they would be blessed and would prosper in the land. But if they didn't obey, the consequences would come in the form of an invading army. Babylon, they concluded, was the ultimate curse that Moses had spoken of. By being in exile in a foreign land, they were paying the price for the sins of their people.[14]

This realization brought them great hope.

They concluded that if there was a penalty for failing to be a kingdom of priests and a holy nation, and they were paying that penalty with their suffering in Babylon, then at some point they would be done paying the penalty.

The suffering would have to come to an end.
They would have done their time and the debt would be paid.
At some point they would be able to say, "It is finished."[15]

Isaiah spoke of their hope this way: "Speak tenderly to Jerusalem, and proclaim to her that her hard service has been completed, that her sin has been paid for."[16]

By the rivers of Babylon, the prophets began to reimagine grace. They started to see what it would look like for Israel's debt of sins to be paid. And what they saw was a reconciling grace so big, so universal, that it could bind all human beings into a brand-new way for the divine and the human to relate.

But the prophets didn't stop there.

If Sinai was supposed to have been a sort of marriage, and that marriage didn't work out, then there would need to be some sort of new marriage between the divine and the human.

A new marriage, which would actually be a remarriage, because the first one fell so far short of what God had in mind.

The prophet Hosea understood all of this history, insisting that God was "going to allure her" and "lead her into the wilderness and speak tenderly to her."[17]

He's telling the exiles that God is going to marry Israel again.

Isaiah puts it like this: "Your husband ... the LORD will call you back."[18]

And then in another place, Isaiah says, "As a bridegroom rejoices over his bride, so will your God rejoice over you."[19]

Which takes us back to Sinai, because the wedding centered around a covenant, a way for God and these people to relate to each other. And the first covenant revealed how unfaithful people can truly be.

So when the prophets spoke of this remarriage, they insisted that something fundamental in the way people related to God would have to change.

The prophet Jeremiah picked up on this, promising that "it will not be like the covenant I made with their ancestors when I took them by the hand to lead them out of Egypt."[20]

The first covenant, the one at Sinai, was terrifying. It involved so much fire and smoke and thunder that the people said, "Moses, you speak to us, because if God speaks to us, we will die."[21]

Jeremiah insisted that the new marriage will be totally different: God will put the truth "in their minds and write it on their hearts."[22]

No more fear,
no more terror,
no more thunder.

That was the old way,
the former thing,
the first covenant.

That was all part of the first marriage that didn't last.

But in the new exodus, the one in which everything will be different than it was before, the truth will be so deeply etched into people's consciousness that they will naturally do the right thing.

New exodus people,
remarried to God,
leaving exile,
headed home.
Home to Jerusalem.

Which raised a few concerns for the prophets.

They understood the danger of returning and rebuilding Jerusalem just as it was before, a political nation-state with armies and palaces and slaves and a temple just like the previous regime. That wouldn't be a "new thing."

That's always the danger, isn't it?

That we'll be broken,
our empires will collapse,
we'll cry out for help,
and when that help comes,
when we get back on our feet,
when there's money in our account again,
and things are back to how they were,
the danger is that once we get it back—
whatever "it" is—
we'll forget what just happened.

And so the way, the prophets insisted, would lead back to some sort of *new* Jerusalem.

The prophet Zechariah said that God would "dwell in Jerusalem," which "will be called the City of Truth."[23] Isaiah promised that "they will beat their swords into plowshares and their spears into pruning hooks. Nation will not take up sword against nation, nor will they train for war anymore."[24]

Truth, peace—a new kind of Jerusalem.

The old Jerusalem had been known for the temple that Solomon built there. This wasn't lost on the prophets.

They promised that even the temple would be transformed in this new reality.

Ezekiel wanted people to "consider its perfection."[25]

Isaiah described just what that "perfection" would be: "They will bring all your people, from all the nations, to my holy mountain in Jerusalem"[26] and "the mountain of the LORD's temple will be established as the highest of the mountains; it will be exalted above the hills, and all nations will stream to it."[27]

What does Isaiah say will happen in Jerusalem? There will be a temple big enough for the whole world to worship in.

A temple big enough for the whole world? Are we reading Isaiah correctly? How could a city, let alone a temple, ever be big enough?

Zechariah answers, "Jerusalem will be a city without walls because of the great number of people and animals in it."[28]

No bricks, no stone, no walls.

But the prophets didn't stop here.

A new exodus,
a new way,
a new marriage with a new covenant,
a new city,

with a new temple, one big enough for the whole world to worship together in—
what's left for the prophets to promise?

What's left is love.

Isaiah says in chapter 19 that "in that day there will be an altar to the Lord in the heart of Egypt," and "it will be a sign and witness to the Lord Almighty in the land of Egypt."[29]

Egypt, according to their ancestors, was the enemy, the oppressor. So what's an altar doing *there*?

"So the Lord will make himself known to the Egyptians, and in that day they will acknowledge the Lord."[30]

Imagine Isaiah's first audience wrestling with these promises. Our worst enemy will become our brothers and sisters in peace?

But Isaiah isn't finished: "In that day there will be a highway from Egypt to Assyria. The Assyrians will go to Egypt and the Egyptians to Assyria."[31]

Assyria was another of Israel's worst enemies. Assyria and Egypt formed an axis of evil for Isaiah's people. And here he's promising that the two nations will have peace with each other. And what will be the bond that brings them together?

"The Egyptians and Assyrians will worship together."[32]

Their bond will be the worship of God?

Isaiah continues, "In that day Israel will be the third, along with Egypt and Assyria, a blessing on the earth. The LORD Almighty will bless them, saying, 'Blessed be Egypt my people, Assyria my handiwork, and Israel my inheritance.'"[33]

Is God serious?

They'll have peace between them?
The three of them will have a meal together?
They'll get along?

These nations hate each other. These are Israel's absolute worst enemies on the planet. For Isaiah's listeners, Assyria and Egypt are the ultimate examples of evil. These are the people Isaiah's audience think need to be wiped off the face of the earth. These are the ones who need to be hunted down and sent a message.[34]

And Isaiah insists that someday they are all going to sit down together in a relationship of mutual respect and love and peace?

Isaiah keeps going, promising "salvation" that reaches "to the ends of the earth."[35]

And what will that salvation look like?

God "will create new heavens and a new earth."[36]

Heavens and earth? That's the language of Genesis.
God is going to do that again?
Bring order out of *this* chaos, the chaos that we know the
world to be today?
A new heaven and a new earth?

Isaiah continues, "The wolf and the lamb will feed
together."[37]

Generally, the wolf eats the lamb. That's how nature
works. The new reality that Isaiah imagines would
somehow involve everything relating to everything else in
a new way. Instead of one eating the other, they will rest
together.

Isaiah's predictions sound like a return to Eden, yet Eden
itself has been transformed. Isaiah even uses the word,
saying that God "will make her deserts like Eden."[38]

The former things didn't work. But the new thing? The
new thing will be different. Bigger, wider, ultimate.

God is going to lead all of creation out of the Egypts of
death and decay and violence? Everything?

For the prophets in exile, no vision was too large, no
dream too big, no hope too beyond what would happen
in the new exodus.

A movement bigger than any one nation, bigger than any
one ethnic group, bigger than any one religion—all of
which raises the question, Who will lead it?

The first exodus was led by Moses, who spoke to the Israelites about their present but also spoke to them about their future. He told them they wouldn't always journey in the wilderness, but someday they would arrive in the Promised Land, they would become powerful and then they would forget God, they would lose the plot and suffer the curse of consequences, and eventually they would find themselves in exile, and after that exile, after the price had been paid, then Moses promised them that "the Lord your God will raise up for you a prophet like me from among you."[39]

Another leader, like Moses.

But the prophets didn't stop there. As they continued to reflect on their history, they realized that their real need wasn't for another Moses; the leader they needed would have something to do with Solomon.

Because he's where it all went wrong. That son of David did not use his power properly. Instead of using it to bless and empower the poor and oppressed, he used his power to coerce people into forced labor to build his empire even bigger.

And so central to the vision of the future, and the identity of the needed leader of the new exodus, was that this leader would be a son of David, but a new son of David who used power purely and properly.

No violence.
No arms dealing.
No palace-building with slaves.

Isaiah calls him a "Prince of Peace" and predicts that he'll "reign on David's throne ... upholding it with justice and righteousness ... forever."[40]

Isaiah connects this coming savior with the failed empire of Solomon. The queen of Sheba had used these exact words, "justice and righteousness," in her explanation of why Solomon had been given so much wealth and power.[41]

It is out of this expectation, about a leader who would use power purely, that a particular word arose to describe this coming one. Isaiah called him a "servant."[42]

This was a radical premise. A powerful leader and ruler who would be a "servant"?

Isaiah said that he'd have the Spirit of God on him and would "proclaim good news to the poor."[43]

Of course, because that's what a servant would do, one who used power purely and properly, that kind of servant would help the poor.

Isaiah records God saying, "See, my servant will act wisely."[44]

Once again, notice the connection to Solomon. The story of Solomon began with his being given wisdom to rule,[45] which he abused as his heart was led astray and he was unfaithful to God. But this servant, the one who will lead a new exodus, "will act wisely." The prophet Jeremiah echoes this, saying that he will "do what is just and right in the land."[46] And then Jeremiah adds, "David will never fail to have a man to sit on the throne of the house of Israel."[47]

Why does he say, "David will *never* fail"?

David himself was told something similar much earlier: "Your house and your kingdom will endure *forever* before me; your throne will be established *forever*."[48] And then Ezekiel claimed that God had predicted, "David my servant will be their prince *forever*."[49]

The prophets started with the assertion that another son of David was coming, one who would use power purely and lead a new exodus, but then something happened in their predictions.

They grew.

They enlarged and expanded.

What started as predictions about an earthly ruler exploded into an expectation of a divinely sent servant who would in some powerful new way rule forever.

This "forever" dimension to the leader of the new exodus wasn't a new idea to the Israelites. There were traces of this in their story. In the book of Genesis, Adam and Eve were promised that one was going to come who would crush all evil once and for all. The serpent who lied about the consequences of eating the fruit was told that a child was coming and "he will crush your head."[50] Deep in the DNA of these people in exile by the river was an anticipation of a coming "serpent crusher" who would liberate all of humanity.

But Israel's failed marriage to God had never produced that child.

And so when Isaiah says, "Sing, barren woman, you who never bore a child; burst into song, shout for joy, you who were never in labor," he's speaking of a coming child, one who will be the result of the union between the divine and the human.[51]

Isaiah isn't just talking about a baby being born. He's talking about something missing, a barrenness in the womb of humanity. The promise is so poignant because from the beginning, from the first moments when our primal ancestors began longing for a way out of this mess we're in, the ache had centered around the birth of one who would crush evil forever.

Here,
by the river,
in exile,

all of these expectations began to coalesce into one
person:

a servant,
a prophet like Moses,
a prince of peace,
a way out of exile.

What began as hope for a Jewish leader for Jewish
people needing an exodus from exile in Babylon evolved
over time into the expectation of a leader who would be
for everybody.

What started as a promise of hope for a particular group
of people beside a particular river turned into a universal
hope for all of humanity, whatever river they find
themselves beside.

And this is how the Hebrew scriptures, also called the Old
Testament, end.

With all of these suspended promises,
hanging there,
unfulfilled,
undone,
waiting.

A group of people by a river who have lost it all, asking
the questions,

What if we had it all back?
What if we could do it again?
What would we do differently?
What if a child was born and a son given?
What if David had *another* son?

CHAPTER THREE

DAVID'S OTHER SON

Egypt.
Sinai.
Jerusalem.
Babylon.

After years in exile, a significant number of Israelites eventually do come home to Israel. They return to Jerusalem, rebuild its walls, and construct another temple.

But when those who had seen Solomon's temple see the new one, they're heartbroken, because it's nothing like its former glory.[1] Things just aren't what they were.

They're not in Babylon anymore. They're now home, but it isn't what it used to be. The Roman Empire, the superpower of their day, conquers Israel and begins a long, oppressive occupation of their nation. Instead of being hauled away to a foreign land by a conquering army like before, this time a foreign army has come to them. Roman soldiers march through their villages, ordering people to carry their packs while taxes are collected so the Romans can build an even bigger army to conquer more nations.

The Romans even build a military center called the Praetorium next to the temple in Jerusalem. They build it a few feet taller than the temple, just to remind the Jewish people who really is in charge when they go to worship their God.

Imagine growing up in a Jewish family in Israel and being taught from your earliest days that your people were chosen by God to be a light to the world.

Imagine going to the synagogue every Sabbath and saying prayers and hearing texts read about your God, the one true God who created all things.

And imagine going to Jerusalem for the festivals and gathering with thousands of other Jews and singing together the great songs of David about the days when things were better.

Songs about victory,
songs about the power of your God,
songs about all of the nations bowing down to your God.

Imagine growing up with that history, that heritage, that story, and then trying to explain to your children just what these Roman soldiers, who don't even believe in your God, are doing in the streets of your village.

This is Israel at the beginning of the first century. Occupation, oppression, shame, and humiliation.

A nation of people wondering where their God is, asking, Why is this happening to us again?

Home, and yet still in a sort of exile.

Clinging to the suspended promises of the prophets, looking forward to the day, the day of hope, the day when another son of David would come and lead them in a new exodus.

Which takes us back to Egypt.

It's written in the book of Exodus that when the Israelites were finally freed from their slavery in Egypt, they had been there four hundred and thirty years.[2]

Which takes us back to Babylon.

The end of the exile could be marked by Nehemiah's return to Jerusalem around 430 BC.

Four hundred and thirty years in Egypt, and then comes Moses.

Four hundred and thirty years back home in Jerusalem, but still in some form of exile.

Four hundred and thirty years hoping that God will restore the kingdom of Israel.

Four hundred and thirty years with the boots of the enemy still on their necks.

And after four hundred and thirty years ... Jesus is born.[3]

Now, there are four versions of Jesus's story in the Bible—Matthew, Mark, Luke, and John—but there's only one quote from the Hebrew scriptures that they all begin with, Isaiah 40:3: "Prepare the way for the LORD, make straight paths for him."[4]

Of all the ways the writers of the Gospels could choose to begin the story of Jesus's going public, they all quote Isaiah 40:3 and the announcement of the new exodus.

A Canaanite woman cries out to Jesus for the healing of her suffering daughter. She calls him "Son of David."[5]

A blind man cries out for Jesus, calling him "Son of David."[6]

A beggar cries out, and how does he get Jesus's attention? By calling him "Son of David."[7]

Jesus hears the beggar's cry. In fact, Jesus hears everyone's cry, even the cry of Canaanites.

David's son Solomon couldn't hear their cry. But this son of David isn't like Solomon.

When the suffering, the sick, and the blind call out "Son of David," it's as much a question as it is a cry.

Which kind of son of David are you, Jesus?

The kind who maintains justice and righteousness, or the kind who builds military bases?

Can you hear us, or are you like Solomon?

The poor and forgotten of Jesus's day use this volatile term "son of David" because of all the emotion and history surrounding it. Just to say the name was to drag up all of the pain of exile and oppression and failure, and at the same time all of the hope and longing and suspended promises that hung in the first-century air.[8]

And where does this new son of David do his first miracle? According to John's version of events, Jesus turns water into wine at a wedding.[9]

A celebration of a marriage covenant?

Weddings in the scriptures were about Sinai, about the union of the divine and the human, about heaven and earth coming together. And it's here, at a party celebrating a man and a woman coming together, that Jesus provides enough wine that the banquet can last for a very, very long time.

Isaiah had talked about wine.[10]

A new son of David, leading the people into a remarriage with God. This is what the prophets had promised. And now it's happening.

A child has been born and a son has been given.

Get down your harps. The day you've been waiting for has come.

And then, early on as well, Jesus leads two of his closest disciples up to the top of a mountain.

Remember, a mountain is where Moses and God talked. And on the mountain, Jesus's disciples see him talking with Moses, along with another of the great prophets, Elijah. And they talk about the exodus, "which he was about to bring to fulfillment at Jerusalem."[11]

Here is the new son of David,
one who can hear the cry of the oppressed,
and he's inaugurating a new marriage covenant
as he leads them in a new exodus.

At one point Jesus even says, "I am *the way*,"[12] which is a new exodus term.

Isaiah spoke of "the way."[13] That's *how* people will return home from exile: they will follow the way.

And this new exodus will be brought to fulfillment in Jerusalem.

Luke tells us again and again that Jesus is headed to Jerusalem.[14]

But it's a different kind of Jerusalem.

Yes, Jesus is headed to a literal city with real streets and houses and a real temple. But he keeps declaring that his ultimate intent transcends the earthly city. He tells a woman in Samaria that "a time is coming when you will worship the Father neither on this mountain nor in Jerusalem."[15] Jesus is very clear that the future, the result of the thing that he is doing, will lead to everybody worshiping in some sort of city, and in some sort of temple that is simply bigger and wider and larger than the kind of temples they were used to—some sort of temple that could hold the whole world.

Jesus goes into the temple area and announces that "one greater than the temple is here,"[16] which Ezekiel had predicted.[17] And now this Jesus is owning up to the prediction, insisting that it is all in the process of coming true through something he is doing right here, right now—in this place, with these people.

Jesus keeps insisting that a new kind of kingdom is "coming,"[18] and he's forever explaining to his hearers what this kingdom is "like,"[19] that it is "upon you,"[20] and that it is "near."[21]

Jesus speaks of a new kingdom as he shows what it's like to be human in this new reality. He heals the sick, gives sight to the blind, helps the lame walk.[22] The prophet

Isaiah had said that the coming servant would do things like this, showing what a new humanity would look like. When John the Baptist sends his disciples to find out about Jesus, he puts his question in the language of the coming exodus: "Are you the one who was to come?"[23]

Jesus answers by pointing to Isaiah: "Go back and report to John what you hear and see: The blind receive sight, the lame walk, those who have leprosy are cleansed, the deaf hear, the dead are raised, and the good news is proclaimed to the poor."[24]

Power is flowing through Jesus to the broken, blind, and lame—those who need it the most, who have no power. Jesus is a servant who uses his power in the service of compassion and love—that's what a servant does.

Isaiah had said this would happen.[25]

A son of David,
who uses power purely,
leading a new exodus,
showing the way to a new city and a new temple,
displaying a new humanity.

Matthew reports that at Jesus's baptism, as he came out of the water, the Spirit of God descended on him "like a dove."[26] This takes us back to the opening lines of Genesis, where it's written that the Spirit of God hovered over the waters of chaos before the work of creation began. The word "hovered" is also used to describe the sound a bird's wings make.[27]

In Genesis, God enters into the primordial waters and out of them begins the work of creation.

Matthew wants us to see that through Jesus, a new creation is coming into being.

John echoes this, beginning his account of Jesus's life with the phrase "in the beginning."[28] This is how the Bible starts. With the creation poem of Genesis explaining how everything came to be—everything.

These writers want their audience to connect what Jesus is doing in first-century Israel with the creation of the world. The first creation was out of chaos. And now Jesus is entering into the chaos of the world, bringing about a new creation.

The writers want to make it very clear that this new son of David isn't just leading a new exodus for a specific group of people; he's bringing liberation for everybody everywhere and ultimately for everything everywhere for all time.

Jesus claims that his message will be preached "in the whole world"[29] and it will be a "testimony to all nations."[30]

Jesus promises that when he's lifted up, he will "draw all people"[31] to himself.

Jesus teaches his followers that "all things"[32] have been committed to him by God.

Jesus insists that his work will lead to a renewal of *all things*.

The "whole world," "all nations," "all people," "all things" are the biggest, widest, deepest, most inclusive terms the human mind can fathom. And they are on the lips of Jesus, who is describing himself.

Anticipation grows as Jesus travels from town to town, village to village, teaching and healing and comforting and explaining and announcing that God is doing something new, something big, and that God is doing it through him. Massive crowds listen to him, people give up everything to follow him, children line the streets and sing about him as the new son of David.

And then it's over.

Jesus is arrested.
And tried as a criminal.
And then killed.
On a Roman execution stake.

Luke tells the story of two of his disciples heading home after his death.[33] They're walking from Jerusalem to Emmaus, the village they left to follow him.

How embarrassing.

Can you imagine returning to your hometown after having made an error in judgment that large? Dropping everything to follow a man because you thought that he was something that apparently he wasn't?

As the disciples walk, they're joined by another traveler, who asks what they are discussing. One of them responds, "Are you only a visitor to Jerusalem and do not know the things that have happened there in these days?"[34] They're shocked that someone could be that out of it. They explain that they had thought Jesus was the one the prophets had promised, the one spoken of in exile who would lead a new exodus. But he was recently sentenced to death and then crucified.

They add that some of Jesus's disciples claim to have gone to his tomb and found it empty, and that others say a risen Jesus has appeared to them, but some friends checked it out and didn't see Jesus. As far as they're concerned, the whole thing is turning into an odd ending to a heartbreaking life. Their despair comes from their hope that "he was the one who was going to redeem Israel."[35]

It's not hard to see why. He follows the predictions of the prophets down to the last word.

He embraces the term "Son of David."[36] He openly acknowledges that he knows exactly what he's doing. He heals people in public. He debates the religious leaders on the finest points of what this coming leader will do and who he will be.[37] And he never stops talking about being a servant.[38]

When the stranger they're walking with hears their perspective, he responds, "How foolish you are."[39] He doesn't empathize with them in their pain or say he understands how hard it is. He thinks they're being foolish.

The stranger continues, "And how slow to believe all that the prophets have spoken!"[40]

Slow and foolish.

His frustration with them isn't that they believed what the prophets had said about Jesus and now his death throws a wrench in *that* plan. His frustration is that they *haven't* believed what the prophets had said about Jesus.

He asks them, "Did not the Messiah have to suffer these things and then enter his glory?"[41]

For these disciples, Jesus's death is the end of hope. For their fellow traveler, Jesus's death isn't the end of hope; it's actually the beginning of hope.

The stranger then explains why Jesus had to suffer, "beginning with Moses and all the Prophets."[42] For the man on the road, everything about the cross and the crucifixion and the death of Jesus can be explained in the Hebrew scriptures.

So what did he say to them? What did he teach them? How did he explain Jesus's death as redemptive and not futile? Did he teach them about violence?

What we see just in the first several chapters of Genesis is what we've seen throughout human history: the misuse of power, which always leads to the escalation of violence.

From Cain on, we've seen how violence escalates until all of civilization is in trouble. The human propensity for bloodshed has been with us from the beginning.

If evil always takes some form of violence, then more violence isn't going to solve anything.

On the night Jesus was betrayed, a group of soldiers come with swords and clubs to arrest him, which is, of course, absurd. But this is how it is with those addicted to the myth of redemptive violence.[43] They come with swords and clubs because it's the only language they know how to speak. Jesus's disciples are outraged, and one of them takes out his sword and starts swinging. Jesus tells him to put away his sword, "for all who draw the sword will die by the sword."[44]

Of course. We've seen enough of that in human history. We know that story.

Jesus then reminds his disciple that he could call on his Father, who would give him whatever military assistance he needs, "but how then would the scriptures be fulfilled that say it must happen in this way?"[45]

It's as if Jesus says, "If I do it like everybody has done it since the beginning of time, how would that change anything?" How would that bring about any sort of new day?

He understands how easily it can go the wrong way, and then we're back in the same old rut, clinging to the notion that violence can bring peace.

The only way to break that cycle is for someone to absorb it. A true leader of a new exodus would have to resist ever using power in the form of violence against another human being.

Isaiah called the one to come a suffering servant.[46]

Someone would have to have the courage to put away the sword, forever, regardless of the consequences for his own security. No matter how tempting it is to pick it up and start swinging, someone would have to say, "Forgive them, Father, because they just don't get it."

If the suffering servant wasn't willing to go the whole way to death without using any violence, if he resorted to the same methods as so many others throughout history did, he'd be just another despot with blood on his clothes.

Is that how the stranger interpreted Jesus's death? As the ultimate cost the suffering servant was willing to pay so that the endless cycle of violence could be broken?

Or did the stranger on the road teach them about exile? Not just Jewish exile but human exile. Not just exile from Israel but exile from Eden.

Cain moved east, away from the garden. And we've been moving east ever since. Everything is in bondage to decay and slavery; the whole cosmos is in a sort of Egypt.

Everything is drifting east.

Moses had told the people that if they weren't true to the covenant, if they failed in the "if" part, there would be consequences.[47] A penalty to pay. The prophets picked up on this, insisting that the exile was that payment.

So if all of creation is in a sort of exile,
east of Eden,
estranged from its maker,
far from home,
what's the penalty for that?

What would be the payment to end *that* exile?

The prophets had declared that someone would come who would be willing to pay that price, the price for all of creation breaking covenant with God. And if that price was paid, that would change everything. Everything and everybody could then come home.

Did the stranger explain to them that the recent public execution of Jesus *was* that price?

Or did the stranger talk to them about Adam?

What has been needed from the start is another Adam, not an Adam who would again give in to the temptation of the serpent but one who would crush the serpent. But the serpent-crusher's victory would have to happen in a specific way. The only way it would actually change things would be if the serpent-crusher survived death—to experience the worst a human can suffer and then come out the other side, alive.

Violence, exile, payment—whatever the stranger on the road taught these disciples from Moses and the Prophets, they got it. Their eyes were opened. The suffering and death and crucifixion of Jesus made sense to them.

In a couple of hours,[48] using nothing but the Hebrew scriptures, this man converted all of their despair to hope and a vision of a new future.

They stopped for food, and "their eyes were opened and they recognized him, and he disappeared from their sight. They asked each other, 'Were not our hearts burning within us while he talked with us on the road and opened the scriptures to us?'"[49]

In Jesus's day, people could read, study, and discuss the scriptures their entire lives and still miss its central message.

In Jesus's day, people could follow him, learn from him, drop everything to be his disciples, and yet find themselves returning home, thinking Jesus had failed.

Which is a bit like walking with someone for hours, only to discover that you had missed who they really are the whole time.

Because the stranger is, of course, Jesus.

CHAPTER FOUR

GENITAL-FREE AFRICANS

Egypt.
Sinai.
Jerusalem.
Babylon.

And on to another man on the road leaving Jerusalem, a man named Philip.[1]

Like most early followers of Jesus, Philip was a Jew. He followed strict rules about what you could and couldn't eat; serious observance of the Sabbath; faithful attendance at the religious feasts in Jerusalem; prayers every day. Extensive laws about what you could touch, what you couldn't touch, who you could touch, who you couldn't touch.

And then Philip met Jesus, and everything changed.

Philip left his everything to follow Jesus, and now he's on a road leading out of Jerusalem, where he meets a eunuch.

A eunuch who's leaving Jerusalem.

This encounter, this direction, this movement away from Jerusalem, is in many ways the story of the early church. Much of this story is written by Luke in the book of Acts, which opens with Jesus, "after his suffering," speaking to his disciples for "forty days ... about the kingdom of God."[2]

And notice where Jesus did this?

On the Mount of Olives.

Remember, Sinai was a mountain.
And "forty" was the number of years the people wandered in the wilderness,
and a "kingdom" of priests was God's desire in Exodus 19, and "suffering" was what Moses said in Deuteronomy 30 had to happen so that the penalty could be paid for infidelity and the people freed for a new exodus.

This moment between Jesus and his disciples is loaded with references to Moses and the exodus. Luke wants us to see that there is a new Moses here, and this new Moses is leading a new exodus.

Jesus tells his disciples, "You will receive power when the Holy Spirit comes on you; and you will be my witnesses in Jerusalem, and in all Judea and Samaria, and to the ends of the earth."[3]

Being "witnesses in Jerusalem" isn't that much of a stretch—that's where the disciples are at the moment. Judea and Samaria make things more complicated, because the Judeans and the Samaritans hated each other. There was great division and animosity between these two regions. Judea was known for its strict religious piety and Samaria for its compromised religious customs. And Jesus mentions them together.

So whatever happens in Jerusalem, or maybe we should say "if" it happens, will somehow lead to the healing and reconciliation of these two regions that are at each other's throats.

It's as if Jesus says, "If it happens in Jerusalem, it will be impossible for it to stay in Jerusalem." But Jesus is not done. After the Judea and Samaria part, he concludes with "and to the ends of the earth."

The prophets had spoken of the "ends of the earth,"[4] because they understood just how global and powerful this message is. If it's liberation for all of humanity, for all of creation, how could something that massive, that true, that good, that compelling stay in Jerusalem?

Luke tells us that the eunuch is reading from the book of Isaiah while leaving Jerusalem, and the eunuch wants to know *who* Isaiah is talking about in a particular passage.[5]

The eunuch wants to know more about Jesus.

Luke also tells us that the eunuch is headed home, to Ethiopia.

In Africa.

Africa is, in the conservative Jewish world of a man like Philip, "the ends of the earth."

Someone from the ends of the earth is asking questions about the new exodus in Isaiah as he heads home.

Now, this isn't the first time Luke has told a story like this. In Acts, he writes that after Jesus's ascension, "when the day of Pentecost came, [the first followers of Jesus] were all together in one place."[6]

And Sinai was about covenant, about commitment, about a group of people at the foot of the mountain agreeing to be the flesh-and-blood representation of God to the world.

The union of the divine and human.

Sinai was the invitation to be a kingdom of priests and a holy nation.

Sinai was where God gave the people the teaching, the way to live in their postslavery reality.

Sinai was ultimately about the whole world returning to the God they had been estranged from since the first people were asked by God, "Where are you?"

There is a Jewish tradition that says the whole world was silent at Sinai, "not even a bird chirped,"[7] as everybody everywhere heard the voice of God inviting humanity into connection with its maker. The ancient rabbis spoke of tongues of fire that went out to all the nations so all people could hear this divine voice in a language they could understand.[8]

So when first-century Jews living in Jerusalem celebrated Pentecost, they gathered together to read the account of Sinai from the book of Exodus and then reflect on the history of their people.

Luke tells us that it was during Pentecost, when the first followers of Jesus were gathered together remembering Sinai, that "they saw what seemed to be tongues of fire that separated and came to rest on each of them. All of them were filled with the Holy Spirit and began to speak in other tongues as the Spirit enabled them."[9]

This is like Sinai all over again, only this time God isn't taking up residence in a tabernacle or a mountain or a set of words. God is dwelling in people.

And this isn't just any group of people; it's people from "every nation under heaven."[10]

It's Parthians,
Medes and Elamites;
residents of Mesopotamia,
Judea and Cappadocia,
Pontus and Asia,

Phrygia and Pamphylia,
Egypt
(Egypt!)
and parts of Libya near Cyrene;
visitors from Rome;
Cretans and Arabs.[11]

The disciples are amazed at and overwhelmed by this
new reality in which everybody everywhere can
understand the new thing that God is doing through
Jesus.

Stunning.

And then Luke adds a significant line at the end of the
story that is easy to miss. He tells us that some people
saw this, the rebirth of Sinai, and made fun of them,
saying, "They have had too much wine."[12]

Aren't there other stories in the scriptures in which the
people had plenty of wine? Where do people drink lots of
wine?

Of course, at weddings. A wedding is where Jesus did his
first miracle, involving wine. And Sinai is also seen as a
wedding ceremony. And it's here at Pentecost that the
church, the bride of Christ, takes her place in redemptive
history and a massive number of people join the Jesus
movement. Luke even tells us how many. And as with
many of the things Luke writes, it's about something else.
We're told that at Sinai, Moses spent so much time up on
the mountain that the people became restless and built a

golden calf to worship instead. When Moses discovered this, he was enraged and called for the death of those who sinned, which a group of Levites carried out in a bloody, murderous act of violence. It's written in the Exodus account that three thousand were killed that day.[13] And how many does Luke say were added to the disciples' number here in the early days of the church?

Three thousand.[14]

Luke wants us to know that Sinai has not been forgotten. The covenant is alive. What was lost is being reclaimed. The divine and the human are coming together again.

God's desires for humanity are thriving.

There's a body of people putting flesh and blood on the divine, and it's called the church. And it's not just about the reclaiming of Sinai, but the speaking in other languages takes us all the way back to the Tower of Babel, where foreign tongues were introduced that threw people into confusion because they were unable to understand each other. The outcome at Babel was the global sociological consequences of human rebellion.[15] The story of the people building a tower reflected the growing human awareness that if technology and power and resources aren't handled with great care and wisdom, all of humanity will suffer. And now, in Jerusalem, at the celebration of Sinai and the inaugural ceremony of the church, people are not being divided by difference but are being united by the Spirit.

People from all over the world understanding each other.

And on a road
leaving Jerusalem,
we have an African
asking questions about Jesus,
hearing the significance of Isaiah's words explained
in a language he can understand.

It makes so much sense to the eunuch that as he and Philip pass a body of water, the eunuch asks if he can be baptized. This question about baptism takes us back to Egypt, to Moses's leading the Israelites through a body of water, which is referred to as the baptism of Moses.[16] The water symbolized their death to the old and their birth in the new, the movement from bondage to freedom.

Baptism is a picture of exodus.

And the eunuch wants to be baptized. His exact words are, "Look, here is water. What can stand in the way of my being baptized?"[17]

Lots of things, actually.

Remember Philip's background and the conservative religion of his time?

According to the law, a eunuch is excluded from the assembly.[18] The law is very clear on that point. As a Jew, Philip should have viewed the eunuch as "damaged goods" and refused to baptize him on that basis.[19] If Philip baptizes the eunuch, he will be breaking a serious rule. A rule that determined your standing with God.

This is the tension throughout the early church.

What do you do when your religion isn't big enough for God?

What do you do when your rules and codes and laws simply aren't enough anymore?

What do you do when your system falls apart because the new thing that God is doing is better, beyond, superior, more compelling?

This isn't just a tension for Philip; it's one of the central struggles of the early church. For many of the first followers of the Way, Jesus was wrapped in layer upon layer of Jewish culture, custom, and lifestyle.

A Jewish messiah,
from the line of the Jewish king David,
raised by Jewish parents
in a Jewish region
of a Jewish nation.

For Philip, the eunuch's question about baptism raises a far deeper set of questions about what it even looks like to follow God.

One of the first Christians, a man named Paul, confronted this tension again and again in the early days of the church. We first meet Paul (whose name originally was Saul but is changed to Paul after he meets Jesus) in Acts 9 when he's "breathing out murderous threats against the LORD's disciples," getting permission from the high priest "so that if he found any there [in Damascus] who belonged to *the Way* ... he might take them as prisoners to Jerusalem."[20]

Damascus is a city in Syria.
Damascus isn't in Jerusalem.
It's beyond Jerusalem.
It's beyond Judea and Samaria.

Paul's concern is that this gospel of Jesus may have left Jerusalem and maybe even Judea and Samaria—it may have even gotten as far as Syria.

Which is what Jesus had said would happen.

And Paul wants to arrest any followers of the Way in Damascus and bring them back to Jerusalem. Paul wants the gospel to travel in the opposite direction from the direction Jesus gave his disciples. Paul wants to bring it back, so that it can't go to the ends of the earth.

But on the way to Damascus, Paul has a blinding encounter with Jesus, one that changes him. He's told to "get up," which is a subtle allusion to the prophet Ezekiel,[21] and then he's taken by the hand to Damascus, where he makes contact with followers of the Way, who are, naturally, terrified of this man who had presided over the killing of followers of the Way.

But Paul is not who he was, and over time people realize that something profoundly transforming has happened to him. One of them is convinced that Paul is going to take the message to "the Gentiles and their kings and to the people of Israel."[22] He's Jewish, born and raised in Cilicia, trained in Jerusalem, fluent in Greek, versed in the customs of Moses, schooled in the philosophers and poets of the day—he's as global as they come.

In Acts 15 Luke writes, "Certain individuals came down from Judea to Antioch and were teaching the believers: 'Unless you are circumcised, according to the custom taught by Moses, you cannot be saved.' This brought Paul and Barnabas into sharp dispute and debate with them."[23]

What's this sharp dispute about?

First, notice the direction. These "certain individuals" were coming from Judea to Antioch. Antioch was one of those non-Jewish ends-of-the-earth type of places. The kind of place that Jesus had told his disciples the message would eventually go. And it has gone there. People are responding to the gospel in Antioch and joining the Way.

But now these religious people are coming from Judea to Antioch, telling these new followers of Jesus about the old religious rituals they're going to need to go through to be legitimate in God's eyes. They use the phrase "according to the custom taught by Moses." They're still stuck in the old covenant, the old way. And not only are they still stuck back there, but they're propagating it.

They're spreading the wrong gospel in the wrong direction.

And it makes Paul furious. In one letter, his rant reaches such a pitch that he says he wishes "they would go the whole way and emasculate themselves!"[24]

It makes him furious because, for Paul, there are two fundamental modes of existence, two pervasive and ultimate realities in which humanity exists: the old condition of darkness and sin and slavery, and the new reality of light and forgiveness and freedom.[25]

In his letter to the Romans, Paul calls the old condition "the body of sin,"[26] which is the dark side of human existence, the resident evil, the sin and death that exist in the cosmos to which human beings are subject. And in another place in Romans he calls it the "body of death."[27]

Many read the word "body" and immediately think of our individual, physical bodies. It's natural for us, then, to assume that Paul is teaching us something here about how to live good, moral lives free from sin. And yes, in a certain sense that is what he's talking about.

But that's not his primary point. Paul uses the phrase "body of sin" or "body of flesh" in a very communal Jewish sense to refer to the reality of the sinful mode of existence of all humanity. It's the realm and reality of the powerful's fearful coercion of the weak, whether they're using tanks and bombs or "the customs of Moses." It's anywhere that power is misused.

And that's what's happening in Antioch. These people are hearing of Jesus and the new exodus and are responding with a yes. They're joining the church, they're learning of the new reality in Christ, and new life is surging through them. And then these religious leaders who are still trapped in the old reality come from Judea and tell them that unless they take part in the religious customs of Moses, none of their newfound freedom means anything.

Paul sees their insistence on a reversion to the customs of Moses as a form of violence.[28] What he's against is religious rituals that replace the freedom, the liberation, brought by Christ. When people are manipulated with guilt and fear, when they are told that if they don't do certain things they'll be illegitimate, judged, condemned, sent to hell forever—that's violence.

It doesn't matter what spiritual language is used or what passages in the Bible are quoted, it's destructive. It's the misuse of power. And central to the way of Jesus is serving, which is the loving use of whatever power you possess for the good of another.

Paul continually returns to his conviction that there are two fundamental modes of existence: the body of sin and the body of Christ. And the Way is the medium of transport from one to the other—the ultimate exodus of humanity.

For Paul, this sharp dispute in Antioch is about the deepest cosmic dimensions of the message of Jesus.

He's convinced that in Jesus, Egypt has been left behind.

Who would ever want to return?

Paul uses new exodus language again in his second letter to the Corinthians, insisting that, in regard to sin and death, through the way of Jesus we have "come out from them."[29]

"Coming out" is what happened when the slaves left Egypt. They came out. And as a result of coming out, they found themselves in a whole new reality of freedom, a reality in which the forces of Pharaoh and slavery no longer held sway over them.

Freed from the Egypt within,
redeemed from the body of sin,
joined to the body of Christ.

Paul writes to the Corinthians that if "the new creation has come: The old has gone, the new is here,"[30] and to the Galatians he writes that "neither circumcision nor uncircumcision means anything; what counts is the new creation."[31]

New creation.

For Paul, this goes all the way back to Genesis, to the creation of the world. There is a new creation, one brought into being through the death of the old and the resurrection of the new, and everybody everywhere can be a part of it.

Which takes us back to the road leaving Jerusalem, to Philip, standing there trying to decide whether to baptize this eunuch from Africa. Philip would have been circumcised when he was eight days old, as all good Jewish boys were. That's one of the ways you took part in the covenant, the one that established and affirmed your relationship with God. Philip would have been taught that circumcision was an absolute, a necessity, something that must be done to be in good standing with God.

But what about the eunuch? Something that the religion of Philip's day held as central to life with God is irrelevant for this African standing before him, for obvious reasons.

You can't mess with the goods if you don't have any.

This is the story of Acts,
the story of the early church,
the story of the Jesus way as it left Jerusalem and
headed to the ends of the earth.

It's the story of a thousand little everyday decisions these first Christians made to free the message from its cultural and religious trappings so that it would truly be good news for all who encountered it.

Peter, another of the first Christians, had an experience similar to Philip's. A Roman centurion invites him to his house, and when Peter walks in, the place is full of the centurion's relatives and friends.[32]

Gentiles. People who aren't Jewish.

Peter tells them, "You are well aware that it is against our law for a Jew to associate with Gentiles or visit them."[33]

Associate with or visit them? Seriously?

This is how severe the religion of Philip and Peter was. You were forbidden to go into the house of someone who wasn't Jewish.

But Peter has been changed, he sees things much differently than he used to, and so he says to the packed house, "But God has shown me that I should not call anyone impure or unclean."[34]

Everything's changing.

Circumcision doesn't count anymore.

You can go into the home of a Gentile.

You can even say to an African eunuch by the side of the road, "Yes, I'll baptize you."

Which is what Philip does.

The gospel is leaving its former confines, Luke wants us to know, and it's heading to the ends of the earth. And that means nothing looks like it used to.

And this takes us back to Philip on the road, leaving Jerusalem. Luke does not tell us how Philip was traveling, whether by foot or horse or donkey, but he does tell us how the eunuch was traveling.

The eunuch was traveling by chariot.

Pharaoh, an African, had chariots.
Solomon bought and sold chariots.
In the scriptures, the chariot is a symbol.
A symbol of empire.
A symbol of oppression and violence.
A symbol of wealth used in the priority of preservation.

In the Psalms, it's written that "some trust in chariots and some in horses, but we trust in the name of the LORD our God."[35]

But this chariot, this chariot is different.

This chariot is not being used for war. This chariot is not being used for violence or coercion or oppression.

This chariot is being used to transport somebody who has just heard the Jesus message and said yes.

Isaiah said that in the new exodus, weapons would be transformed for better purposes—"swords into plowshares"[36] is how he put it.

And now it's happening.

This little detail Luke includes is far more significant than just a truth about chariots; it's a truth about empire.

Because that's always the temptation, isn't it? To build and accumulate at the expense of others. Jesus's earliest disciples struggled with this when he first told them that they would be witnesses in Jerusalem, Judea, and Samaria, and to the ends of the earth. Their question had been, "Are you at this time going to restore the kingdom to Israel?"[37]

Jesus has been telling the disciples about the kingdom of God—the realm, the reality, the way in which the weak are put first and the widow and the orphan and refugee are remembered and "justice and righteousness" are upheld, as the queen of Sheba would say.[38] But the disciples aren't asking about *that* kind of kingdom. Their question is about another kind of kingdom. They want to know if the old kind of kingdom is going to return, the one with horses and military bases and palaces. Their question is essentially, "Are you now going to pick up the sword and start swinging, purging our land of the Roman Empire so that we can have our privileged status as God's people back?"

They still don't get it.

They want to take back their nation for Jesus.

They want to return to the regime of their founding fathers.

They want a renewed empire with their ideology on the throne.

They're still holding on to the distorted hope that Jesus is going to reconstruct the same old broken system, only this time they'll be the ones calling the shots and holding the prime cabinet positions.

But Jesus is inviting them to participate in a reality so liberating and compelling that Jerusalem can't contain it. The disciples can't fathom something that new and transcendent.

Jesus urges them to consider "something for everybody," but their question is about what the future will look like for them. Their question about kingdom shows that they have confused blessing with favoritism.

The central promise to the father of their faith, Abraham, was that God would bless his people so that they would bless the world.[39] It's always about wealth, health, possessions, and influence being used to bless others. But the disciples' interest isn't in the ends of the earth. They're interested in regaining the kingdom of comfort they once had. They long for the blessing of God for themselves. Deep in their bones is the belief that they are God's favorites. For them, blessing is about favoritism. We are chosen and elect and favorite; therefore we deserve certain securities and benefits.

They're still trapped in the entitlement of the old covenant religion.

We see this belief in the fact that eight chapters after Jesus tells them to go to the ends of the earth, Luke writes that beginning with the martyr Stephen's death, "a great persecution broke out against the church in Jerusalem, and all except the apostles were scattered throughout Judea and Samaria."[40]

There was a problem; the gospel hadn't left the confines of Jerusalem.

But then persecution broke out, and they scattered—to the very places Jesus wanted them to go all along.

Sometimes it takes a little pain to get us to do the right thing.

And not only does the gospel begin to leave Jerusalem, but so do Africans in chariots.

Luke gives another detail about the eunuch: he is in charge of the treasury of the queen of Ethiopia.

Now, the chariot detail was significant, but the eunuch's job?

That's huge.

He's in charge of the wealth of one of the empires of the nations. And he's just been baptized, he's said yes to the new exodus, and he's joined the Jesus movement.

The wealth of the nations, entrusted to a Jesus follower.

That was the problem in Jerusalem, wasn't it?

The misuse of wealth.

The building of palaces and terraces and a temple using slave labor.

But this African official has glimpsed a new reality, and everything changes.

We see the economic dimensions of the new exodus again and again in the early church. On the heels of the story of the languages and the three thousand being added to their number, we're told that they "were together and had everything in common. They sold property and possessions to give to anyone who had need."[41]

Instead of building towers and forcing others to make storehouses out of bricks so that some are stockpiling while others are slaves, this new movement is ruled by generosity. And compassion. And sharing. The gospel for these first Christians is an economic reality. It's holistic and affects all areas of their lives. It's an alternative to the greed and coercion of empire.

It's a whole new order of things.

And what does Paul do everywhere he goes?

He takes an offering for the poor.[42]

He never stops reminding people of their responsibility to use their wealth and power purely and properly, for the benefit of those who need it the most.

And now a eunuch who controls massive wealth is headed home, having joined the way of Jesus. The wealth of the nations, being harnessed for the good of humanity. Isaiah had said this would happen.[43]

Luke writes that the eunuch "went on his way rejoicing."[44]

Acts is a story of movement,
motion,
progress.

It's people being caught up in something that simply must expand,
and stretch,
and go.

Because no one city,
no one religion,
no one perspective,
no one worldview can contain it.

In Acts 13 the church leaders are gathered together worshiping when the Spirit of God leads them to set apart Barnabas and Paul for specific work they've been called to do.

"Set apart" takes us, again, back to Sinai. God had given instructions to "set apart" the mountain[45] as the place where he would meet the people, then "set apart" Aaron and his sons,[46] then "set apart" the objects in the temple,[47] then "set apart" themselves.[48] Being set apart was about God's desire to have a people who would show the world the divine.

But it isn't just about setting apart Paul and Barnabas; Luke says it happened "while they were worshiping."[49] The Greek word for worshiping here is *leitourgio*. It's where we get the word liturgy. The word is sometimes translated "worship," other times "service."

Worship and service.

So which is it?

The answer is yes. Both.

And this is important because worship and service are what a priest does.

The priest's work, the priest's *service*, was understood as an act of worship. This was God's desire at Sinai—that everybody would understand their role as priests. That everybody would worship God by serving each other. That those wouldn't be two things, but one. This is why God continually mentions the widow, the orphan, and the refugee. Remembering them, caring for them, serving them *is* worshiping God. But the people stood at a distance and essentially said, "Can't someone else do it?" They hadn't lived up to their priestly calling. Isaiah picked up on this and said that in the new exodus, the one for all of humanity, one of the things that would happen is "you will be called priests of the LORD."[50]

This passage in Acts 13 is the first time in human history when a group of people has fully embraced the invitation given at Sinai. There is a direct line from Exodus 19 to its first fulfillment here. This is the first time in redemptive history when the gathered people of God join together as willing priestly agents to the world.

Paul understood the historic significance of this moment, writing to the church in Rome that he's "a minister of Christ Jesus to the Gentiles. He gave me the priestly duty of proclaiming the gospel of God."[51]

And when we last see Paul, at the end of Acts, he's in Rome, the gateway to "the ends of the earth," the city where all roads lead. He has gathered with the Jewish leaders and "witnessed to them from morning till evening."[52]

The word "witnessed" takes us back to the first chapter of Acts, to Jesus telling his first followers that they'll be witnesses. Paul is now with the Roman Jews "explaining about the kingdom of God, and from the Law of Moses and from the Prophets."[53] And from Moses and the Prophets is, of course, how Jesus explained himself to the disciples on the road to Emmaus.

Paul is gathered with the religious leaders, trying to "persuade them about Jesus." He doesn't first go to the Gentiles; he goes to the religious faithful, he attends their gatherings, he speaks to them in their language. Paul does this because he knows that if the church gets converted, the whole world will follow.

And then Luke wraps up the story of Acts: "For two whole years Paul stayed there in his own rented house and welcomed all who came to see him. He proclaimed the kingdom of God and taught about the LORD Jesus Christ—with all boldness and without hindrance!"[54]

Luke ends his account with Paul, miles from Jerusalem, at the center of a thoroughly non-Jewish world, sharing the message with whoever is interested.

He "welcomed all who came to see him."

All.

That's who this Jesus is for.

Even soaking-wet genital-free Africans riding home in chariots.

CHAPTER FIVE

SWOLLEN-BELLIED BLACK BABIES, SOCCER MOMS ON PROZAC, AND THE MARK OF THE BEAST

Early in the morning of March 19, 2003, several planes took off on a bombing mission to inaugurate a U.S. military effort called Iraqi Freedom. The target was a palace compound called Dora Farms. It was believed that the Iraqi president, Saddam Hussein, was staying there, that the bombs would kill him, and that American military objectives would be met. The pilots spoke of how stunning the new weaponry was that they had at their disposal, making it clear that these particular missiles— four enhanced two-thousand-pound satellite-guided "bunker busters"—cause virtually no collateral damage. Around 5:30 A.M. they fired their missiles as they flew over the compound before heading back to their base.[1]

At a press conference soon afterward, the U.S. secretary of defense said, "The weapons that are being used today have a degree of precision that no one ever dreamt of in a prior conflict."[2]

A doctor working at a hospital near Dora Farms had a different perspective: "Honestly, what we saw the first day of the war astonished us.... There were shrapnel injuries to women and children, civilians.... We didn't receive any soldiers.... All of them were civilians who were in their houses at dawn."

The missiles missed their target. They landed on homes nearby filled with Iraqi civilians. A camera crew filming the removal of the bodies from the remains of the houses came across a man whose son and two nephews were in one of the houses. Sitting among the rubble, the man said, "Due to this behavior, America will fail. She will fail completely among the countries. And another country will rise and take America's place. America will lose because her behavior is not the behavior of a great nation."

She will fail?

Completely?

America will ... lose?

Now, some would point out that this man was clearly overcome by grief and mourning and was in no position to make claims about the future of a nation on the other side of the world.

Others would respond by speaking of the complexities of modern warfare. Yes, it's tragic this man suffered like this, but that's one of the unfortunate costs of the greater good of removing Saddam Hussein from power.

Others might point out that this is what happens when you live next to the palace of a violent dictator who has slaughtered untold thousands of innocent people to further his destructive purposes.

And then there are some who would respond to his prediction by emphasizing all of the great things about America. Because the world has never seen anything like America. What was an idea, an experiment, an attempt at a new kind of nation, went from being a few small colonies to *the* superpower in a little over two hundred years.

Astonishing.

They would remind us of all of the people who have come to the United States for life, liberty, and the pursuit of happiness and have actually found them.

They would speak of advancements in technology, the arts, medicine, humanitarian aid. They would point out that it's hard to find a corner of the world where there aren't Americans doing some sort of good.

They would point to the many who have sacrificed their lives so that we could enjoy the freedom and prosperity that we do. And they would be right. These things should be pointed out and celebrated and honored.

Besides, America is powerful. And it's hard to get more powerful than a two-thousand-pound missile.

Which takes us back to the man on a rant in the rubble next to Dora Farms. It's at the height of a display of shock and awe that this man sees failure.

What is going on here?

That question takes us back to a road, a road leading away from Jerusalem back to a small village called Emmaus.

What we saw on that walk with Jesus and his disciples is that it's possible to be with Jesus every day and yet miss who he truly is and where we really are. The disciples' response to the events surrounding his death was to ask, "Are you only a visitor to Jerusalem and do not know the things that have happened there in these days?"

They have a particular perspective on current events and have no sense that they may have entirely misinterpreted them.

Do you not know about the war on terror?

Do you not know about militant, fundamentalist Islam and its desire for world dominance?

Do you not know about the need for homeland security?

Do you not know that Jesus was just crucified in Jerusalem?

Jesus knows.

Not only does Jesus know, but he has an entirely different understanding of what just took place in Jerusalem, an understanding that strikes to the core of their entire worldview, and in the process of explaining to them what's really just happened, he reaches out to save them from perpetuating the very thing he came to save them from.

So with a cross jammed into the pile of rubble at Dora Farms and the man's cry ringing in our ears, let's listen with fresh ears to the Bible. Because what's going on here is an ancient phenomenon known as empire.[3]

America is an empire.

And the Bible has a lot to say about empires.

Most of the Bible is a history told by people living in lands occupied by conquering superpowers. It's a book written from the underside of power. It's an oppression narrative. The majority of the Bible was written by a minority people living under the rule and reign of massive, mighty empires, from the Egyptian Empire to the Babylonian Empire to the Persian Empire to the Assyrian Empire to the Roman Empire.

This can make the Bible a very difficult book to understand if you are reading it as a citizen of the most powerful empire the world has ever seen. Without careful study and reflection, and humility, it may even be possible to miss central themes of the scriptures.

Because what's true of empires then is true of empires now.

What we see in the Bible is that empires naturally accumulate wealth and resources.

Solomon built terraces and stockpiled gold.

America controls nearly 20 percent of the world's wealth.[4] There are around six billion people in the world, and there are roughly three hundred million people in the United States. That makes America less than 5 percent of the world's population. And this 5 percent owns a fifth of the world's wealth.[5]

One billion people in the world do not have access to clean water, while the average American uses four hundred to six hundred liters of water a day.[6]

Every seven seconds, somewhere in the world a child under age five dies of hunger,[7] while Americans throw away 14 percent of the food we purchase.[8]

Nearly one billion people in the world live on less than one American dollar a day.[9]

Another 2.5 billion people in the world live on less than two American dollars a day.[10]

More than half of the world lives on less than two dollars a day, while the average American teenager spends nearly $150 a week.[11]

Forty percent of people in the world lack basic sanitation,[12] while forty-nine million diapers are used and thrown away in America *every day*.[13]

One point six billion people in the world have no electricity.[14]

Nearly one billion people in the world cannot read or sign their name.[15]

Nearly one hundred million children are denied basic education.[16]

By far, most of the people in the world do not own a car.[17]

One-third of American families own three cars.[18]

One in seven children worldwide (158 million) has to go to work every day just to survive.[19]

Four out of five American adults are high school graduates.[20]

Americans spend more annually on trash bags than nearly half of the world does on all goods.[21]

Now, when many people get a glimpse of how the world really is, whether it's through travel or study or reading statistics like the ones just cited, it can quickly lead to guilt. We have so much, while others have so little.

Guilt is not helpful.

Honesty is helpful. Awareness is helpful. Knowledge is helpful.

Guilt isn't.

Human history has never witnessed the abundance that we consider normal. America is the wealthiest nation in the history of humanity. We have more resources than any group of people anywhere at any time has ever had. Ever.[22]

God bless America?

God has.

And we should be very, very grateful.

Empires accumulate. And that accumulation has consequences. Blessing and abundance can turn into burdens and curses.

The number of Americans taking antidepressants has tripled in the past decade.[23]

If all of this was supposed to make us happy, why are so many of us so sad?

But not everybody is sad. There is another response to accumulation, and it's called entitlement.

Moses spoke of the need to constantly tell the exodus story, the one about rescue from slavery, "otherwise, when you eat and are satisfied, when you build fine houses and settle down, and when your herds and flocks grow large and your silver and gold increase and all you have is multiplied, then your heart will become proud and you will forget the LORD your God, who brought you out of Egypt."[24]

Moses can see the days of abundance and blessing coming. Someday they will not only have enough, they will have more than enough. And he knows that this blessing is going to bring with it tremendous temptation to forget the God who provided it. How does a person forget God? The answer we've seen again and again in the scriptures is that you forget God when you forget the people God cares about. Over and over God speaks of the widow, the orphan, and the refugee.[25] This is how you remember God: you bless those who need it the most in the same way that God blessed you when you needed it the most.

Moses describes God as the one "who brought you out of Egypt." Everything is connected to their experience of redemption and their extending redemption to others. In an empire of indifference, as it becomes harder and harder to understand the perspective of others, it becomes easier and easier to confuse blessing with entitlement.

Entitlement leads to immunity to the suffering of others, because "I got what I deserve" and so, apparently, did they.

Moses warned about this as well in Deuteronomy 8, when he said, "You may say to yourself, 'My power and the strength of my hands have produced this wealth for me.' But remember the LORD your God, for it is he who gives you the ability to produce wealth."[26]

In an empire of entitlement, when the fundamental awareness is lost that this is all a gift, luxuries can begin to seem like necessities. Excess can become normal. And it can be very easy to lose perspective on just how much we have.

One leader of the American government announced that "the American lifestyle is not up for negotiation."[27] This can sound like a perfectly rational thing to say. It may even sound quite impressive to some, as in, "We won't let anyone push us around." Statements like this can even get a person elected. Because, after all, "we've worked hard and we deserve what we've earned."

But the problem is that for others in our world, this kind of statement is heard in an entirely different context.

Imagine hearing this as one of the three billion people on the planet who survive on two dollars a day.

In the same way that entitlement can cause us to lose perspective, it can also cause us to resist checks on consumption. If a particular resource becomes scarce at home or in other parts of the world, it can be very difficult to cut back, because the powerful forces of entitlement convince us certain things are deserved.

Empires naturally accumulate, accumulation has consequences, and those consequences are expensive.

The three leading oil consumers in the world are China, which consumes 5.6 million barrels a day, Japan, which consumes 5.5 million barrels a day, and the United States, which consumes 20 million barrels a day.

To give a sense of just how much oil that is, if it were lined up in one-gallon cans, it would circle the earth at the equator almost six times.[28]

The United States accounts for 25 percent of global oil consumption while having 3 percent of its reserves.

This is a problem.

In 2001 the United States imported 54 percent of its oil.

This is an even bigger problem.

The oil we need has to be obtained from somewhere else. And one of those somewhere elses is a particular region of the world called the Persian Gulf. Two-thirds of the world's oil supplies are in the Persian Gulf, and in 2002, 20 percent of all oil in the United States came from the Persian Gulf. Among the countries in this region, there is one that has the biggest oil reserves on the planet. It's called Saudi Arabia, and it's a very important country to American oil companies.

Saudi Arabia is also a very important country to quite a few other people in the world for a very different reason. In Islam, there are three places on the planet that are considered the most holy sites. The third most holy site in the world for Muslims everywhere is the city of Jerusalem. The second most holy site for Muslims all over the world is Medina. And the most holy site in the world for Muslims everywhere is Mecca. And both Mecca and Medina are in Saudi Arabia.

The country with the largest oil reserves in the world is Saudi Arabia, and the country with the second largest oil reserves in the world is also in the Persian Gulf, and it's called Iraq.

One American government official said that the United States "must have free access to the region's [Persian Gulf] resources."[29]

Which takes us back to Jerusalem. What we saw with Solomon is that his wealth and abundance naturally led to the priority of preservation. He had to allocate a growing portion of his resources to protecting and securing what he had accumulated. And so he built military bases and bought chariots and horses. This is where the priority of preservation leads: to larger and larger standing armies, stockpiles of weapons, and shows of force.[30] Which cost more and more money. Which have to be maintained with more and more resources. More and more is being spent to preserve and protect the more and more that is being accumulated, and that, of course, requires more and more resources, which, of course, need to be protected and preserved with more and more.

This is the vicious cycle of the priority of preservation.

How much is enough?

The United States accounts for 48 percent of global military spending.[31]

Less than 5 percent of the world's population purchases nearly half of the world's weapons.

In 2008, the United States spent more on defense than the next forty-five countries combined.[32]

The United States spends more on defense than on all other discretionary parts of the federal budget combined.[33]

Human history has never seen a military machine like the American armed forces.

And what has the United States built in Saudi Arabia?

We have built military bases on land considered holy by a significant percentage of the world's population.

Because there's oil there.

And we need that oil.

If you are a citizen of an empire that has the most powerful army in the history of humanity and is currently on the way to spending a trillion dollars on a war, passages in the Bible about those who accumulate chariots and horses from Egypt are passages about you and your people.

When it's written in the Psalms that some trust in chariots and some trust in God, this is a statement about empire and power. It's a contrast between two different ways of being in the world.

Empires accumulate. Accumulation gives birth to entitlement, entitlement demands preservation, preservation has consequences, consequences are a burden.

And that burden takes faith to carry.

In empire, you believe in that which you preserve, you preserve that which you are entitled to, and you are entitled to that which you have accumulated.

This is the religion, the animating spirit, of empire.

And all of this makes it harder and harder to hear the stories of those who don't have this particular faith.

The temptation in an ever-expanding empire is to fail to hear the cries of those who haven't directly benefited from the abundance that the empire has been blessed with. For our Native American neighbors and friends, the birth of our country is deeply connected with the deaths of thousands and thousands of their ancestors. The word for this is genocide. A whole people group was decimated as this land was claimed by its conquerors.[34]

Us.

For many of our African American neighbors and friends, their ancestors were brought here on boats to work as slaves on large Southern plantations that made their white owners very, very wealthy. Which made their country very, very wealthy.

Which has made us very, very wealthy.

At the end of World War II, America dropped two nuclear bombs that killed tens of thousands of innocent people. And we didn't have to. The Japanese were already defeated.[35]

This takes us back to the Bible. What is unique to the biblical narrative is its self-critique. History is usually told by the winners, whose version of events usually focuses on their victories and good deeds. People rarely record their failures and defeats.

But the Bible is different. At the height of Israel's power, while Solomon is reigning at the peak of his glory, we find the most incisive and honest critique of the empire itself. We're told the weight of his gold was 666—which, remember, is a Jewish way of saying that somebody has so profoundly lost their way that they are now acting in opposition to God.[36]

This is a warning to us of the powerful impulse within an empire to tell only one version of the story, the version that glosses over the dark side and the injustices in order to serve the larger story of continued supremacy and success. In an empire, we must be careful not to become indifferent to the cries of those among us, no matter how uncomfortable they make us. When the prophet Isaiah compared the power and wealth of the king's regime to a "hut in a field of melons,"[37] this was not what the king wanted to hear. This did not serve the prevailing propaganda of the kingdom.

The Roman Empire that ruled the world in the time of Jesus was masterful in its repeated telling of one version of its story. A phrase the Caesars often used was "peace through victory." They would come to a region they hadn't yet conquered, announce they were going to make this particular region a part of their empire, and then proceed to occupy it with their army. Anyone protesting this arrangement could quickly find themselves on a cross. For those in the lands being conquered by the massive Roman military muscle, it wasn't peace. It was destruction. Death. The end of life as they knew it.

"Peace through victory" depended on which side of the sword you were on.

There's a theme that occurs over and over in the Bible: God sent the Israelites messengers again and again, but they did not listen.[38]

If the system works for you, it can be quite hard to understand the perspective of people who have the boot of the system on their neck.

If you have the power, it can be hard to understand the voice of those who have no power.

If you have choice, options, and luxuries, it can hard to fathom the anger of those who don't.

If you have always had enough food, it can be hard to understand the shouts of those whose stomachs are grumbling from hunger.

Which takes us back to the road to Emmaus. Whatever Jesus taught these disciples from Moses and the Prophets, it changed their belief about what had just happened in Jerusalem. They had been walking home as followers of Jesus possessing an understanding of the scriptures diametrically opposed to the work of Jesus in the world.

Followers of Christ missing the central message of the Bible? It happened then, and it happens now. And sometimes the reason is, of course, empire.

A tragic example of what happens when Christians miss the central message of the scriptures is the way in which the book of Revelation, the last book of the Bible, is taught and understood in American culture. Revelation is a letter from a pastor named John to his congregation. To understand how significant the letter is, it helps to understand its first-century historical backdrop.[39]

First, the emperor. The Caesars, who ruled the Roman Empire, saw themselves as gods on earth, sent to bring about peace and prosperity. Throughout the first century, the Caesars had taken their divinity more and more seriously, demanding more and more overt displays of worship and acknowledgment from their subjects. Many of them demanded that their subjects worship them as the Son of God, the divine one ruling the earth with the favor of the gods. One Caesar had a choir that followed him wherever he went, singing, "You are worthy, our Lord and our God, to receive honor and glory and power."[40]

Second, economics. The Caesars understood that at the heart of the empire is economics. If you want to truly control people, you need to control their money. So if you went to the market to buy or sell goods, you first needed to give an offering acknowledging Caesar as Lord and that you were an obedient subject of his kingdom. If you didn't, you couldn't take part in the economy, which meant you wouldn't make any money and you'd eventually starve. It is believed that a system was developed to identify who had made the offering to Caesar and who hadn't, and this system involved some sort of mark you received to acknowledge your confession of Caesar as Lord and your ability to take part in the market.

Third, peace. The Roman army would march into a new land or region, one they had not conquered, and announce they were taking over. They would demand that the citizens of that land confess Caesar as Lord. If they refused, they could be killed, often crucified, as a public demonstration of what happens when you defy Caesar. This had a way of bringing people in line with the Roman way.

Fourth, exile. The Caesar in power at the time of John's writing understood just what a challenge the church of Jesus was to his rule. These Christians believed that someone else, someone not him, was the true Son of God and that he alone deserved their worship and acknowledgment of divine status. Caesar believed that the way to get rid of this threat was to send the pastor into exile so that he couldn't lead his people.[41]

Revelation is a letter written from John, the pastor, to his church during his time of exile. He writes in a subversive literary style called apocalyptic. It uses a vast array of symbols and images and stylized language to convey profound truths about how the world works. John refers to a beast, which is his word for the corrupt, destructive system of violence and evil that is pervasive in our world. He writes of a dragon, the one who does the work of the beast on earth. And then he talks about a mark of the beast.[42]

We can assume John's audience knew what the mark was—how you bought and sold in the market. The mark was a symbol of your participation in the military-economic complex of the Roman Empire.

The mark represented an all-encompassing system aligned against people doing the right thing.

The mark spoke to all of the ways humans misuse power to accumulate and stockpile while others suffer and starve.

The mark was anti-kingdom.

And John says don't do it. Don't take the mark. Don't take part in the animating spirit of empire.

Resist. Rebel. Protest.

Revelation is a bold, courageous, politically subversive attack on corrosive empire and its power to oppress people.

The people who read this letter would have been confronted with a fundamental question: Who is Lord?

Jesus or Caesar?

Whose way is *the* way?

The way of violence or the way of peace?

The way of domination or the way of compassion?

The way of building towers to the heavens or the way of sharing our bread with our neighbor?

The way of greed and economic exploitation or the way of generosity and solidarity?

Who is your Lord?

Imagine how dangerous it would be if there were Christians who skipped over the first-century meaning of John's letter and focused only on whatever it might be saying about future events, years and years away. There is always the chance that, in missing the point, they may in the process be participating in and supporting and funding the various kinds of systems that the letter warns against participating in, supporting, and funding.

That would be tragic.

That wouldn't be what Jesus had in mind.

That would be anti-Jesus.

That would be anti-Christ.

Were the people in John's church reading his letter for the first time, with Roman soldiers right outside their door, thinking, "This is going to be really helpful for people two thousand years from now who don't want to get left behind"?

It's a letter written to a real group of people, in a real place, at a real time, enduring excruciatingly difficult times. Christians were being killed by the empire because they would not participate.

John comforts them, challenges them, warns them, teaches them, inspires them—don't take the mark of the beast.

Imagine the average youth group in the average church on the average Sunday. Imagine visiting this youth group and having the pastor say to you, "I just can't get my kids interested in Jesus. Do you have any suggestions?"

How do you respond?

To begin with, the church has a youth group. This is a brand-new idea in church history. A luxury. Everybody in the church doesn't meet all together? All of the babies and older folks and men and women and widows and students aren't in the same room, but they've gone to separate rooms?

And there are resources for this? People and organizational structures and a budget? Let's imagine that in this case, this pastor, this youth pastor, is paid a salary for his or her work. A church with enough resources to pay someone to oversee the students? Once again, this is brand-new, almost unheard of in most of the churches in the world, and in church history, a brand-new invention.

This salary can be paid and this building can be built because people in the congregation have surplus. They have fed themselves and their children and bought clothes and houses, and now, after these expenses, there is still money available. And this money is given in an act of generosity to the church, which disperses it to various places, among them the bank account of the pastor.

In many, if not most, of the churches in the world, immediate needs simply don't allow for such luxuries— too many people are hungry, too many don't have a roof, too many are sick—and so any surplus is spent immediately on the basic needs staring them right in the face,

people dying here,
right now,
today.

But this particular church is blessed, and we should be clear about this—it *is* blessing. It is good. It is fortunate that this particular church doesn't have those issues. This church has enough resources to hire a pastor who had the resources to get training to gather these students in the student room to teach them about the way of Jesus.

Many Christians around the world would simply stand in awe of that kind of blessing.

And the students in this church, these are good kids. They are from families who just want to see their kids become good Christians.

Imagine just how much is available to them. They have more at their fingertips than any generation in the history of the world—more information, more entertainment, more ideas, more ways to kill time, more options.

Many of them own more than one pair of shoes.

There are even some among them who have eaten at least one meal every day of their lives.

So we are talking about a minuscule minority of kids in the world.

At the exit off the highway near their church is a Best Buy and a Chili's and a Circuit City and a McDonald's and a Wal-Mart and a Bed, Bath and Beyond, much like the other towns in their state and in their country. The music they listen to is distributed by one of five major corporations, which also own the movie studios that create the movies they watch, which are also connected to the corporations that create the food they eat and the commercials they watch, which also have significant ties to the clothes they wear and the cell phones they own, and the ring tone on their cell phones, the one by the artist who is signed to the record label that is owned by the same company that owns the cell phone company and the advertising agency that announced the artist's new album, which is owned by the same company that owns the beverage company in whose advertisement the artist appeared, drinking that particular beverage, singing the song that is now a ring tone on the students' phones that they purchased at the mall across the street from the Olive Garden next door to the Home Depot on the other side of the Starbucks.

And so each week they gather to hear a talk from the pastor.

Their pastor tells them about the Jesus revolution.
About Jesus resisting the system.
About the blood of the cross.
About many of the first Christians getting arrested.
About Jesus having dinner with prostitutes and tax collectors.
About people sharing their possessions.
About Jesus telling a man to sell everything.
About the uniqueness of their story in the larger story of redemption.

How do children of the empire understand the Savior who was killed by an empire?

How does a twelve-year-old who has never had hunger pangs that lasted more than an hour understand a story about a twelve-year-old providing fish and bread for thousands of chronically hungry people?

How do kids who are surrounded by more abundance than in any other generation in the history of humanity take seriously a Messiah who said, "I have been anointed to preach good news to the poor"?[43]

How do they fathom that half the world is too poor to feed its kids when their church just spent two years raising money to build an addition to their building?

They gather, they sing, they hear a talk from the pastor, and then they get back in the car with their parent and they go home; the garage door opens up, the car goes in, and the garage door goes down.

This is the revolution?

This is what Jesus had in mind?

And so the youth pastor turns to you and says, again, "I just can't get my students engaged with Jesus. Do you have any suggestions?"

What do you say?

How do you respond?

Your only hope, of course, would be to remind him or her that there is blood on the doorposts of the universe.

CHAPTER SIX

BLOOD ON THE DOORPOSTS OF THE UNIVERSE

Blood on the doorposts of the universe?

In Egypt, today is just like yesterday, and tomorrow will be just like today. Wake up, make bricks for Pharaoh, go to bed. Wake up, make more bricks for Pharaoh, go to bed. An endless cycle of despair. History has stalled. It isn't going anywhere.

Because tomorrow is going to be just like today.

This is where Exodus begins, without hope. And God is nowhere to be found. That is what makes the story of Exodus so compelling. A new day is about to dawn. And it will begin tonight.

Tonight is going to be different.
Tonight the system is going to be subverted.
Tonight the empire will be powerless.

onight the regime will be caught flat-footed.

Because God has heard the cry of the people, and God has come to do something about their oppression.

Moses and Pharaoh have been going back and forth, Moses insisting on freedom and Pharaoh reasserting slavery. Moses demanding liberation, Pharaoh enforcing bondage. And finally, Pharaoh relents.

It's time to leave Egypt.

And so tonight is going to be a night unlike any other.

There are specific instructions on what to do on this night, and those instructions center on a lamb.[1]

Every revolution needs a spark, an icon to capture people's attention, an event that overcomes the despair and atrophy that years of oppression create. And whatever it is, whatever event or figure or symbol sends the people over the edge into their new future, that image becomes the defining memory of the good that has just begun.

People need a catalyst, a symbol, a picture of what freedom will look like. Otherwise, they might keep quiet, they might continue to tolerate the old regime, they just might keep making bricks.

And what would that spark be for Israel? What picture would tell them and generations to come that they were made for freedom?

On the night of the exodus, every Jewish man was instructed to take a lamb "for his family, one for each household," to sacrifice it, and to "eat the meat roasted over the fire ... with your cloak tucked into your belt, your sandals on your feet and your staff in your hand. Eat it in haste; it is the LORD's Passover."[2]

For Israel, the symbol of revolution is a lamb.

A lamb that is slain.
A lamb that is innocent.
A lamb sacrificed for each family, each household.

As the climax of the plagues approaches and Pharaoh's end finally draws near, instead of letting Israel flee wildly into the desert, God tells them to stop, sacrifice a lamb, cover their doorposts with its blood, and share a ritual meal.

And the lamb is to be a substitute for the firstborn of each Jewish household. Whatever divine retribution is about to fall upon Egypt will pass over the households, sparing the firstborn where the blood of the lamb appears.[3]

But why this particular ritual? And why the emphasis on the firstborn? In the culture at this time, the firstborn son served as a representative of the family and took care of all the matters of the family. Therefore, if the lamb redeemed the firstborn, then the whole Jewish household would be saved.

For the Egyptians, the firstborn son of Pharaoh had the same rank as Pharaoh himself. He was a son of the god Ra and would thus carry on the rule of heaven after his father died. This meant that the dynasty depended on the survival of the son more than the father.

In this ancient period, when life and death were subject to the whims of fate, the firstborn son was a form of national security. For Pharaoh and his people, the firstborn son was the sign of the god Ra's ongoing presence with them.

But the God of Israel also had a son.

Moses is instructed to say to Pharaoh, "This is what the LORD says: Israel is my firstborn son, and I told you, 'Let my son go, so he may worship me.'"[4]

Israel is God's firstborn. And through Israel, God's intention is to show the world what God is like. God wants to redeem all of humanity through the firstborn son, Israel.

God's judgment, then, on the firstborn of Egypt is a declaration that the gods behind Pharaoh's brutal and oppressive rule are powerless and will be allowed to tyrannize humanity no longer.

Pharaoh is being judged. Plagues have brought the world's superpower to its knees, but before the journey can begin, there's a meal.

A meal unlike any other.

And central to this Passover meal is the command never to forget it. The people are told to set aside the date and make it the beginning of their calendar, because time will now be marked by this event.

"When your children ask you... then tell them, 'It is the Passover sacrifice to the LORD, who passed over the houses of the Israelites in Egypt and spared our homes when he struck down the Egyptians.'"[5]

A lamb sacrificed for the people becomes the flash point for God's revolution. Blood on the doorposts of the house of Israel.

This event took on significance later, as the exiles in Babylon made connections between their situation and their ancestors' slavery in Egypt. As the prophets painted bigger and wider pictures of what the new exodus would look like, they realized that all of creation was in a sort of exile. And for all of creation to leave exile and come home, it would take more than the blood of an innocent lamb.

Sin would have to be dealt with in an entirely new way.

The prophets described a suffering servant, a firstborn child among God's firstborn nation who would take upon himself the burden not only of Israel's exile but of the exile of all of humanity.

Isaiah said that a firstborn son of Israel would emerge and he would be despised and rejected, a man of suffering, and familiar with pain. The suffering he would endure would be such that people would hide their faces from him; he would take the pain and suffering of others upon himself. He would not look like the powerful rulers of empire but would be considered punished by God, stricken and afflicted.[6]

The prophet Isaiah promised that someday, suffering and exiled Israel would produce a suffering servant who would not be spared. This sacrificial lamb would be a man, a firstborn son, and he would take the path not of violence and coercion but of sacrifice.

Just before the birth of Jesus, Joseph returned to Bethlehem, "the town of David, because he belonged to the house and line of David," where Mary "gave birth to her firstborn, a son."[7]

Jesus the lamb,
but a different kind of lamb.

A son of David,
but of a different kind.

God's firstborn.

John the Baptist understood this, declaring, when he first saw Jesus, "Look, the Lamb of God, who takes away the sin of the world!"[8]

And what does Jesus do on the night he's betrayed and arrested? He has a Passover meal with his disciples.

And it's at this meal,
the Passover meal,
that he takes the bread and says, "This is my body,"
and then he takes the cup and says, "This is my blood."[9]

Jesus takes the ritual remembrance of that night unlike any other and he makes it about *himself*.

He's about to be arrested, put on trial, and then hung on a cross to die. He knows this. He knows where this is headed.

This time the firstborn will not be spared. This time the lamb is God's own Son and no substitute will be given. The cup will not be taken away from him.

For Jesus, his coming death is about the new exodus. Betrayed by a friend, a victim of injustice and cruelty at the hands of religion in collusion with empire, God's Son chooses the path of a lamb.

In the first exodus, the lamb's blood was placed on the doorposts of the house for the salvation of the Israelites who lived there. In the new exodus, Jesus's blood is about something bigger.

Paul describes Jesus as "the firstborn," but not the firstborn of a single household. Not the representative of a people suffering in Egypt. Paul describes Jesus as "the firstborn over all creation."[10] The blood of this lamb is about something far bigger. Jesus is the representative of the entire human family. His blood covers the entire created order. Jesus is saving everyone and everything. Jesus is leading all of creation out of the Egypt of violence, sin, and death. All that was lost at the garden, in exile east of Eden, is being redeemed in the act of this firstborn son.

And our response to this? In the scriptures, it's written again and again that we are to remember and be thankful.

The Greek word for thankful is from the verb *eucharizomai:* the Greek word *eu*, which means "well" or "good," and the word *charizomai*, which means "to grant or give." It's from this word that we get the English word Eucharist, the "good gift." Jesus is God's good gift to the world.

On the cross, Jesus's body is broken and blood pours out for the healing of the world. As it's written in Colossians, on the cross, through the blood of Jesus, God is reconciling to himself all things.[11]

God has made peace with the world through the Eucharist, the good gift, of Jesus. And so Christians take part in a ritual, a meal, a reminder of the Passover, called the Eucharist—also called Communion or the Lord's

Supper or Mass—as a way of remembering and returning to who God is and what God has done in Christ.

But the Eucharist, as it is with any ritual, is about something far more significant than the ritual itself.

Paul writes to his friends in the city of Corinth, "We are hard pressed on every side, but not crushed; perplexed, but not in despair; persecuted, but not abandoned; struck down, but not destroyed."[12]

It's clear that things have been difficult for Paul, but he doesn't get bitter, he doesn't complain, and he doesn't lose hope.

Instead, he says, "We always carry around in our body the death of Jesus, so that the life of Jesus may also be revealed in our body."[13]

Jesus allowed his body to be broken and his blood to be poured. And so Paul is allowing his body to be broken and his blood to be poured. Now, some of this is literal— he actually was beaten and flogged until he bled. But he's speaking of something deeper. He's speaking of a whole way of life. He has committed himself to a cause larger than himself—he's planting churches, he's taking offerings for the poor, he's traveling from city to city teaching and giving spiritual direction to those who need it.

And it's hard. It costs him something.

He's criticized, he gets tired, he gets frustrated, he's betrayed, his heart is broken again and again.

Paul continues in his letter, "For we who are alive are always being given over to death for Jesus's sake, so that his life may also be revealed in our mortal body."[14]

The "given over" is important here. Paul is speaking of the healing of the world and how when we identify with the suffering of our neighbor and we commit ourselves to doing something about it, it will cost us something.

He continues, "So then, death is at work in us, but life is at work in you."[15]

How can the death that is "at work in us" produce "life" in his friends?

That's how the Eucharist works.

For someone to receive, someone has to give.

For someone to be fed, someone has to provide the food.

If someone is inspired, which means that life has been breathed into them, then somebody else had life breathed out of them.

If someone somewhere benefits, then someone somewhere has paid something.

God gives the world life through the breaking of Christ's body and the pouring out of Christ's blood. And God continues to give the world life through the body of Christ—who Paul tells his friends at Corinth is them.

They are his body. The body of Christ.

The church is a living Eucharist, because followers of Christ are living Eucharists.

A Christian is a living Eucharist, allowing her body to be broken and her blood to be poured out for the healing of the world.

In 1 Corinthians 9 Paul writes that "to the Jews I became like a Jew," and then "to those under the law I became like one under the law," and then "to those not having the law I became like one not having the law," and then he concludes with "to the weak I became weak."[16]

There's a glaring absence in his list. The opposite of being "under the law" is "*not* being under the law." The opposite of weak is … Paul doesn't mention it.

After the "to the weak I became weak" part he should have said "and to the strong I am strong."

But he doesn't say that.

He doesn't say he's become strong to those who are strong.

He only says he's become weak to the weak.

If you've ever been to an Alcoholics Anonymous meeting, you know what this is like. An AA meeting is a room full of people who are done pretending. There are no facades. There is no acting. And it's overwhelmingly powerful. Everybody in that room is in recovery from addiction, and they all know each other's games, masks, and manipulations. A whole world of posturing and pretending is simply absent. You're there because you have hit bottom, at least most of the time, and you need others who know how it feels.

Writer Anne Lamott says that the most powerful sermon in the world is two words: "Me too."

Me too.

When you're struggling,
when you are hurting,
wounded, limping, doubting,
questioning, barely hanging on,
moments away from another relapse,
and somebody can identify with you—
someone knows the temptations that are at your door,
somebody has felt the pain that you are feeling,
when someone can look you in the eyes and say, "Me too,"
and actually mean it—
it can save you.

When you aren't judged,
or lectured,

or looked down upon,
but somebody demonstrates that they get it,
that they know what it's like,
that you aren't alone,
that's "me too."

Paul does not say, "To the strong I become strong." He only says, "To the weak I am weak."

Paul understands that the power of the Eucharist comes from its weakness, not its strength.

Later he writes to the Corinthians, "Who is weak, and I do not feel weak?"[17] At the heart of the church, in the soul of the Eucharist, is identification with the suffering of another human being.

To begin to understand the Eucharist, to begin to grasp the Father's giving of the firstborn son, is to feel what others feel, to suffer when they suffer, to rejoice when they rejoice. The church says to the world, "Me too."

Us too.

There is a truth here, deep in the heart of the Eucharist, that transcends the polarities of strength and weakness, isolation and identification, loneliness and solidarity.

In the temple in Jerusalem, everything was arranged spatially. In the center was the temple itself, containing the Holy of Holies, where it was believed God was present in a unique way. Outside of the temple building itself was the court where the priests performed their sacrificial duties. Outside of the priests' court was the court of the Jews, where the average Jewish worshipers gathered. Outside of that was the outer court for the Gentiles, the non-Jewish worshipers. If you were in the court of the Gentiles and you wanted to go into the court of the Jews, you were confronted by a wall separating the two courts, and on the wall was an inscription that informed you that if you were a Gentile and you went into the court of the Jews, you would be killed.

Subtle.

This, of course, had a powerful effect on people, especially Gentiles. Because it was believed that God is in the center, and the closer you get to the center, the closer you're getting to God.

Paul writes to the Ephesians, a mixed group of Jews and Gentiles and slaves and masters and men and women and Greeks and Romans, that Jesus "himself is our peace, who has made the two one and has destroyed the barrier, the dividing wall of hostility, by setting aside in his flesh the law with its commands and regulations."[18]

In his flesh?

Jesus's death, the breaking of his body and the pouring of his blood, is for Paul an end to a whole system of "commands and regulations." And among those commands and regulations is the wall in the temple that divided the one group of people, the Jews, from the other group of people, the Gentiles.

That wall, which he calls a wall of hostility, has been destroyed. That whole old way of thinking and doing things is simply irrelevant. Jesus has made peace. And the reason he's done this? "His purpose was to create in himself one new humanity out of the two, thus making peace, and in one body to reconcile both of them to God through the cross, by which he put to death their hostility."[19]

Peace has been made.

A church is where peace has been made.

Because in the Eucharist, in Jesus's body and blood, everything has been reconciled to God. Paul calls this the "new humanity."

The Eucharist is about the new humanity.

People who previously had nothing in common discover that the only thing they now have in common is the one thing that matters.

People who had previously found themselves on opposite sides of a wall find out that the wall has been destroyed.

People who had fought over an endless array of issues realize that peace has been made and there is nothing left to fight about.

In the new humanity,
you hear perspectives you wouldn't normally hear,
you walk in someone else's shoes.

You find out that the judgments you had previously made
about that group of people or that kind of men or that
kind of women or all of those kids simply don't hold up
because now you're getting to know one of "those" and
it's changing everything.

You learn that your labels for different people groups are
insufficient, because people are far more complex and
unpredictable and intelligent and creative.

You used to have a rigid stance on a particular issue, but
now you've heard the other side and it's impossible
anymore to categorize them all as stupid and uninformed
and heartless, because you realize that they have thought
about their position and they have weighed the
consequences and they have some good points that you
must consider.

In the new humanity our world gets bigger, our
perspective goes from black-and-white to color, our
sensitivities are heightened, we're rescued from sameness
and uniformity, because the wall has come down and
peace has been made.

A church is the new humanity on display.

She's in graduate school, and he's in his nineties;

and one couple has a million dollars, and another doesn't have enough money for dinner;

and he arrived in this country three years ago with a small suitcase, and they've never been out of the country;

and they have a son fighting in the war, and they're going to a war protest later today;

and he's got serious doubts about what he was taught growing up, and she's just decided that God might even exist.

All of these people—who are divided, who never sit down and listen to each other—in the new humanity, in the church, they meet, they engage, they interact, they begin to feel what the other feels, and the dividing wall of hostility crumbles.

In the new humanity,
them becomes us,
they becomes we,
and those become ours.

This is why it is very dangerous when a church becomes known for being hip, cool, and trendy.

The new humanity is not a trend.

Or when a church is known for attracting one particular kind of demographic, like people of this particular age and education level, or that particular social class or personality type. There's obviously nothing wrong with the powerful bonds that are shared when you meet up with your own tribe, and hear things in a language you understand, and cultural references are made that you are familiar with.

But when sameness takes over, when everybody shares the same story, when there is no listening to other perspectives, no stretching and expanding and opening up—that's when the new humanity is in trouble.

The beautiful thing is to join with a church that has gathered and find yourself looking around thinking, "What could this group of people possibly have in common?"

The answer, of course, would be the new humanity.

A church is where the two people groups with blue hair—young men and older women—sit together and somehow it all fits together in a Eucharistic sort of way.

Try marketing that.

Try branding that.

The new humanity defies trends and demographics and the latest market research.

In Acts 8 some of Jesus's first followers are healing people, and a man named Simon sees this and offers them money and says, "Give me also this ability."[20]

Simon is seduced into thinking that the movement of the Spirit of God is a commodity to be bought and sold like any other product. The apostles chastise him for his destructive thinking, because the Eucharist is not a product.

Glossy brochures have the potential to do great harm to the body and blood.

Church is people.
The Eucharist is people.
People who have committed themselves to being a certain way in the world.

To try to brand that is to risk commodifying something intimate, sacred, and holy.

A church is not a center for religious goods and services, where people pay a fee and receive a product in return. A church is not an organization that surveys its demographic to find out what the market is demanding at this particular moment and then adjusts its strategy to meet that consumer niche.

The way of Jesus is the path of descent. It's about our death. It's our willingness to join the world in its suffering, it's our participation in the new humanity, it's our weakness calling out to others in their weakness.

To turn that into a product blasphemes the Eucharist.

The Eucharist is what happens when the question is asked, What does it look like for us to be a Eucharist for these people, here and now?

What does it look like for us to break ourselves open and pour ourselves out for the healing of these people in this time in this place?

The temptation is simply to duplicate the Eucharist of someone else.

There are conferences and websites where a church leader can do this. Sermons and plays and songs and mission statements and Bible studies and programs can be purchased and downloaded from a variety of sources.

There's obviously nothing wrong with using what someone else created—it's a beautiful thing to learn from the journey of others. Whenever someone has tapped into the deep stream of the historic Christian faith, whenever a church has stumbled upon the big truths about who Jesus is and what it looks like to be his body, we should celebrate this
and study it
and learn from them
and ask questions
and wrestle with how to apply what they've encountered in their context
to our context,
to our city,
to our neighborhood,
to our church.

But this sharing and learning and exchanging of ideas can never be a substitute for a church asking the difficult questions about its own Eucharist.

The measure of a sermon is not whether it affirms what you already believe. A sermon is not a product to be consumed and then evaluated according to how good it was or whether it was pleasing or enjoyable.

If a sermon can be resolved in the time it took to deliver it, then it missed something central to what a sermon even is, which is connected with what the Eucharist is. The gathering of the church, in a service or worship or teaching setting, is to remind, instruct, and inspire people about being Eucharist for the worlds they find themselves in. It's written in the letter to the Hebrews that they shouldn't give up meeting together because they should "consider how we may spur one another on toward love and good deeds."[21]

The phrase "good deeds" comes from the Hebrew word *mitzvot*,[22] which refers to actions taken to heal and repair the world. It's a concept rich with significance in the Jewish tradition. For the writer of Hebrews, the church gathers so that the body will spur one another on to live a particular way day in and day out.

These gatherings aren't the end; they're the beginning. They're the start. They put things in perspective, they remind, they provoke, they comfort, they inspire, they challenge, but ultimately they are about the Eucharist.

About these people in this place at this time being equipped to be a Eucharist.

The sermon is about starting the discussion. The sermon is about having the first word. The sermon is a catalyst that inspires people into whole new ways of seeing their lives.

The Eucharist is ultimately about what we do *out there*, in the flow of everyday life.

When the goal of a church is to get people into church services and then teach them how to invite people to come to church services, so that they in turn will bring others to more church services—that's attendance at church services.

And church is not ultimately about attending large gatherings.

Church is people, people who live a certain way in the world.

People who have authority in the world, but authority that comes from breaking themselves open and pouring themselves out so that the world will be healed.

The authority that the church has in culture does not come from how right, cool, or loud it is, or how convinced it is of its doctrinal superiority.

As Paul says, "We don't fight with those weapons."[23] A church's authority comes from somewhere else—it comes from how we've been broken open and poured out, not from how well we've pursued power and lobbied and organized ourselves to triumph. This is why when Christians organize politically and start flexing that muscle, making threats about how they are going to impose their way on others, so many people turn away from Jesus.

Jesus's followers at that point are claiming to be the voice of God, but they are speaking the language of Caesar and using the methods of Rome, and for millions of us it has the stench of Solomon.

It's not the path of descent,
it's not weak resonating with weak,
it's not the Way,
it's not Eucharist.

What the Eucharist does is particularize the exodus story in time and space. Exodus is the ultimate picture of salvation.

People in slavery, rescued by the grace of God and brought to a land flowing with milk and honey.

People told to "get up, because this is the night!"

People who were led into a new tomorrow, one unlike today.

People who were then told to leave the corner of their field, the olives they missed on the first pass, the grapes they didn't pick on the first round.

Why were they told to do this?

So that the poor in their midst could pick them up.

People who were told to do this because "I am the Lord your God, who brought you out of Egypt."[24]

How are they taught to keep the exodus, the grace of God, alive in their lives?

By remembering the poor.

When you give unconditionally, you will be reminded of the God who gives unconditionally.

When you extend grace to others in their oppression, you are reminded of the grace extended to you in yours.

The Eucharist is the firstborn, the church leading the way in exodus. Every time we take part in the Eucharist, we're reminded that we were each slaves and God rescued us. The church must cling to its memory of exodus, because if that memory is forgotten,
the church may forget the poor,
and if the poor are forgotten,
the church may forget what it was like to be enslaved,
and that would be forgetting the grace of God.

And that would be forgetting who we are.

Our standing in solidarity with the single parent, the unemployed, the refugee, our joining the God of the oppressed to work for justice in the world, doesn't just make a difference for those who are suffering.

It rescues us.

Have you ever heard someone return from a trip to a third-world setting and talk about how the "people there" have nothing and yet they have so much joy?

Our destiny, our future, and our joy are in the Eucharist, using whatever blessing we've received, whatever resources, talents, skills, and passions God has given us, to make the world a better place. Disconnection from the suffering of the world, isolation from the cry of the oppressed, indifference to the poverty around us will always lead to despair.

We were made for so much more.

The church, the Eucharist, says no to religiously sanctioned despair. The Eucharist is an invitation to be the new humanity. To suffer, to bleed, to open the heart, to roll up the sleeves, to have hope that God has a plan to put the world back together, and it's called the church.

In the Eucharist, there's always hope.

Hope for the poor, and hope for the rich. Hope for the bored, hope for the restless.

The Eucharist confronts its culture with the question, If we can spend a trillion dollars on a war, what else could we spend a trillion dollars on?

Water?
Food?
Medicine?
Education?

The Eucharist is about converting all of that ability and energy and entrepreneurial skill and can-do attitude into blessing for those on the underside of power.

Those on the margins. Those who aren't in the game.

The Eucharist is about people with the power empowering the powerless to make a better life for themselves.

The church says no to the animating spirit of religious empire, the one that leads Christians to look no different than the world around them. Churches can easily become centers for assimilation, where the seats in the sanctuary are eerily similar to the seats in the cinema, the website offers all of the programs to meet your specific religious needs, and the coffee in the hallway is just as good as in the shops across the street.

The church says no because in buoyant, hopeful, passionate embrace it has already said yes to the new humanity.

It's written to the Ephesians that God's "intent was that now, through the church, the manifold wisdom of God should be made known to the rulers and authorities in the heavenly realms."[25]

We have been given everything we need for the fulfillment of the story. And the act of loving the poor is an act of fulfilling, remembering; it's living our hope; it's the fullness of him who fills all things in all ways.

It's not a building, because no building can ever be big enough for that kind of grace.

The Eucharist is not fair.

Giving to those who can't give in return, that's not fair.

Serving those who have no way to serve in return, that's not fair.

Breaking yourself open and pouring yourself out for people who may never say thank you, that's not fair.

Because God is not fair. This is a God who is defined by action on behalf of the oppressed. God is about giving the good gift. Jesus is God's good gift for the healing of the world. The church is Jesus's body, a good gift for the healing of the world.

It's for the benefit of others. For the good of those who look different from us.

A church is an organization that exists for the benefit of nonmembers.[26]

This blessing extends even to our enemies.

This truth about the Eucharist raises profound questions that a church must ask itself. If our church was taken away—from our city, our neighborhood, our region—who would protest?

Only the people who are members?
Only those who are a part of it?
Only those who attend its services?

Single mothers?
Refugees?
Atheists?

Because the Eucharist is, after all, a meal.

We saw Isaiah's declaration that Egypt, Assyria, and Israel would worship together.

Egypt? The enemy?

Assyria? The hated?

If the prophet were to speak to us today, painting pictures of what it will look like when Jesus comes to town, what pictures would he give us?

Who are our enemies today? What would be the modern equivalent of this?

Taliban, my son? Al Qaeda, my beloved?

The Eucharist is about the church setting the table for the whole world.

The Eucharist is about the new humanity.

The Eucharist is about God's dream for the world.

The problem isn't that our buildings are too big and too expensive. Ezekiel spoke of God's dream of a temple that the whole world could worship in. The problem is that our buildings aren't big enough. Bricks and stone and glass and sound systems simply aren't expansive enough for all that God wants to do in our world ...

through the church.

The writer of Hebrews passionately, emphatically announced that through Jesus and the movement he is leading, we have come
to a new mountain,
to a new Jerusalem,
to the church of the firstborn,

and to blood that speaks a better word than the blood of Abel.[27]

Genesis tells the story of God speaking to Cain after he murders his brother and telling Cain that he can hear Abel's blood crying out from the ground.[28]

Cain says, "Am I my brother's keeper?"

The church answers, "Well, actually, Cain, you are."

We all are.

We are all our brothers' and our sisters' keepers.

The Eucharist is saying yes to human community.

Where was God when I tested positive?
Where was God when I was suffering?
Where was God when I lost my job?
Where was God when I was hungry?
Where was God when I was alone?

The Eucharist is the answer to the question.

It's about the freeing of human conscience to experience the total acceptance of God, and it is about human community and its right and longing to be free. It is the way to a universal religion adequate to the challenge of saving human community and the ultimate renewal of all things.

The church is the living, breathing, life-giving, system-confronting, empire-subverting picture of the new humanity.

It's written to the Colossians that God "has rescued us from the dominion of darkness"—that's a reference to slavery in Egypt—"and brought us into the kingdom of the Son he loves, in whom we have redemption."[29]

Jesus has rescued us.

His blood, our redemption.

He's the good gift.

The church says yes to the good gift.

The church is the good gift.

For the world.

Because there's blood on the doorposts of the universe.

BROKEN AND POURED

There's a pattern here—a pattern we find in the story of the Bible that gives us insight into the deepest truths of how the universe works.

Egypt.
Sinai.
Jerusalem.
Babylon.

Salvation is what happens when we cry out in Egypt. Because we all have our Egypts, don't we?

Addiction, suicidal thoughts, anger, rage—we've all got darkness and slavery in our hearts somewhere. Prejudice, hate, envy, lust, racism, ego, dishonesty—we each could make our lists. And they would be long. The wrong and injustice we see around us every day right down to the smallest details involving how we think and feel and act. The Bible uses the word sin for this condition of slavery.

The technical definition of sin in the scriptures is "to miss the mark." We've all missed the mark in some way.

Even deeply antireligious people affirm that something is seriously wrong with our world and that wrong is nowhere more present than in the human heart.

At the center of the Christian experience is crying out in our slavery and being heard by God. Trust that, through Jesus, God has done for us what we could never do for ourselves.

Rescue.

Redemption.

Grace.

This grace takes us to Sinai.

Egypt. Then Sinai.

Sinai is where we find purpose and identity.

God doesn't just want to save us; God is looking for a body, a people to incarnate the divine.

We're invited at Sinai to join the God of the oppressed in doing something about our broken world. And that always involves hearing the cry of the oppressed and then acting on their behalf.

If we forget them, we lose track of our own story.

Our story then takes us from Sinai to Jerusalem. And Jerusalem raises the question,

What will we do with our blessing?
What will we do with all that God has given us?
Will we remember Egypt?
Or will we lose the plot?

And sometimes we lose the plot. We become proud, we start to feel entitled, we allow our abundance to isolate us from who we really are. And we find ourselves in exile, which can be abrupt and shocking. And sometimes exile can be so subtle, we don't realize what's happened until later.

And in exile we can slip into despair,
or we can reimagine everything.

Confession.
Repentance.

A fresh start.
A clean slate.

We cry out in our exile and God hears us and we experience rebirth.

There's a pattern built into the universe; it's true for each of us, and it's also true for groups of people.

In a world in which there are twenty-seven million slaves,[1]

in a world in which 840 million people will go to bed hungry tonight because they cannot afford one meal,[2]

in a world in which one million people commit suicide every year,[3]

in a world in which today nearly 4,500 people in Africa will die of AIDS,[4]

Jesus wants to save our church from the exile of irrelevance.

If we have any resources,
any power,
any voice,
any influence,
any energy,
we must convert them into blessing for those who have
no power,
no voice,
no influence.

Remember what God says to Cain, in between the "What have you done?" part and the "Your brother's blood cries out to me from the ground" part?

God says to Cain, "Listen!"[5]

Because everything begins with the cry.

It begins with someone crying and someone else hearing.

And it's hard to hear the cry when you're isolated from it.

In Proverbs it's written that the rich man's wealth is his "fortified city."[6] People fortify cities with walls meant to keep people out. But the problem with walls is that they also keep people in. Jesus told a parable about a rich man and a man named Lazarus, who was poor and sat outside the rich man's gate each day. The rich man's gate kept Lazarus out, but it also kept the rich man in.[7]

Walls isolate.

So can gates.
And freeways.
And school systems.
And grocery stores.
And health clubs.
And shopping malls.
And homes.
And office buildings.

But when we hear the cry, everything changes.

You can live anywhere, you can work anywhere, but if you hear the cry, everything changes.

Because when we hear the cry, we're with God.

When God gets Moses's attention and lays out for him what liberation is going to look like for his people, he tells Moses to "go."[8]

"Listen," and then, "Go."

The going will take a multitude of forms.

It will be movement,
action,
life.

It will involve risk,
It will mean conversations with people who are nothing like us,
and it will probably involve questions and criticism and perhaps even rejection from people who haven't heard what we've heard.

It's about all of us taking the next step out of Egypt, doing the next right thing, being open to whatever it means for us to be a Eucharist, right here, right now, with what God has given us today.

And whatever it is, it will not be boring. Tomorrow will not be like today. And it will cost something.

The Eucharist always does.

It isn't just about trying to save the world.

It's about saving ourselves.

From the kingdom of comfort.
From the priority of preservation.
From the empire of indifference.
From an exile of irrelevance.

Jesus wants to save our church from thinking that the priests are somebody else.

Jesus wants to save us from standing at a distance, begging Moses to speak to God because we're convinced that if we speak to God, we'll die.

Jesus wants to save our church from fear.

We haven't been brought to that kind of mountain.

Sinai, alive again.

Instead of standing at a distance and saying, "Someone else," it's stepping up and stepping in to the invitation to the risk, to the suffering, to the joy.

And when we listen and go, it will never be about guilt.

It will never come on the heels of "Well, I guess I'm supposed to."

The Eucharist doesn't work like that.

The suffering, the cost, comes from hearing something that rings in your head and heart with such force that you can't stop hearing it.

It comes from being captivated by a great cause—one so massive and compelling that you'd sell everything you have to be a part of it.

God is with us when we go, when we respond, when we hear, when we listen.

We find God in our own oppression, in our own crying out, in our own response to the body of Christ broken for us, the blood of Christ poured out for us, and when we can't find God in our own oppression, we can always find God in the oppression of others.

A converted church will cause the mountains to tremble.

A group of people taking the bread and the cup, asking, "What now, Jesus?"—the stars sing when that happens.

When the church gets saved, the queen of Sheba will be there in moments.

Jesus wants to save us from making the good news about another world and not this one.

Jesus wants to save us from preaching a gospel that is only about individuals and not about the systems that enslave them.

Jesus wants to save us from shrinking the gospel down to a transaction about the removal of sin and not about every single particle of creation being reconciled to its maker.

Jesus wants to save us from religiously sanctioned despair, the kind that doesn't believe the world can be made better, the kind that either blatantly or subtly teaches people to just be quiet and behave and wait for something big to happen "someday."

The Bible begins with Abel's blood "crying out from the ground."

The Bible ends with God wiping away every tear.[9]

No more death, or mourning, or crying, or pain.

Hope. The church is always about this hope. The church is about getting down your harp. The church confronts the religiously sanctioned despair of so many who follow Christ but have settled for a life of exile.

On the night he was betrayed, Jesus led a Passover meal unlike any other. He took the bread and the cup and connected these symbols with himself. He told them to "do this in remembrance of me."[10]

The "do this" is understood to be the taking of the bread and the cup as the body and blood of Christ.

So we take it and we taste. We reflect and remember. We sing and we pray. We take part in this two-thousand-year-old ritual. Some of us "do this" in a church service, some every day, and others with a small group of friends. We "do this" in all sorts of ways and in all sorts of places with all sorts of diversity. Some of us "do this" with chants, and some of us in silence. In some settings a priest or a pastor or an elder or a leader serves us, and in other settings people serve each other, and in other gatherings people serve themselves.

We do this in remembrance of Jesus because the ritual moves us, it changes us, it humbles us, it brings us together.

Just try to do this with someone you are not speaking to. You'll end up reconciling or at least speaking or at least being more understanding and more compassionate.

But what if Jesus meant something else—something beyond the ritual? What if he was talking about our actually enacting what the ritual is all about over and over, again and again, year after year? What if the "do this" he primarily meant wasn't the ritual he was leading his disciples through at that moment. What if the "do this" was his whole way of life?

He has chosen the path of descent; he comes into Jerusalem
on a donkey, not a horse,
with children, not soldiers,
weeping,
humble.

And he dies,
naked,
bleeding,
thirsty,
alone.

Maybe that's what he means when he says, "Do this in remembrance of me." The "do this" part is our lives. Opening ourselves up to the mystery of resurrection, open for the liberation of others, allowing our bodies to be broken and our blood to be poured, discovering our Eucharist. Listening. And going.

Because when we do this in remembrance of him,

the world will never be the same;

we will never be the same.

Now *that* is a manifesto.

ENDNOTES

INTRODUCTION **TO THE INTRODUCTION**

1   Yes, you.

2   Dr. Tom Holland teaches biblical theology at the Wales Evangelical School of Theology in the UK. For further reading, see his *Contours of Pauline Theology* (Ross-shire, Scotland: Christian Focus, 2004) or his forthcoming commentary, *To Love and Hold: The Divine Marriage; A Biblical Commentary on Paul's Letter to the Romans* (Bridgend, Wales: Zephyr, 2008).

3   Matthew 6:1–2.

INTRODUCTION **AIR PUFFERS AND RUBBER GLOVES**

1   Genesis 4:4–5.

2   For a historical-fiction perspective on progress and civilization, read *The Source* by James Michener. It will take forever to read, but it will be worth it.

3 Genesis 4:16.

4 Verse 17.

5 Genesis 11:2.

6 A few examples: scripture says that before things go badly for Lot and his family, he "set out toward the east," where he parted company with Abraham and pitched his tents near Sodom (Gen. 13:11–12). Bad move! In Genesis 25 the place of exile for Isaac's illegitimate half brothers is the east. The text reads, "Abraham left everything he owned to Isaac. But while he was still living, he gave gifts to the sons of his concubines and sent them away from his son Isaac to the land of the east" (Gen. 25:5–6). In Jacob's famous dream, he's promised the land on which he is lying (Gen. 28:10–22), but his faith must first be tested by a journey "to the land of the eastern peoples" (Gen. 29:1).

7 See the movie *Planes, Trains, and Automobiles*: "You're going the wrong way!"

8 Genesis 3:9.

9 Featured on CNN's *The Situation Room* with Wolf Blitzer, April 13, 2007, http://transcripts.cnn.com/TRANSCRIPTS/0704/13/sitroom.01.html.

JAMIE MCINTYRE, CNN SR. PENTAGON CORRESPONDENT: Well, Wolf, as you know, I've flown in the V-22. And I've got to tell you, it's a very impressive plane. Very fast, very maneuverable. But the real test is going to come now as it's sent into combat.

(BEGIN VIDEOTAPE)

MCINTYRE (voice-over): After almost 20 years, and more than $50 billion, the Marine Corps says its revolutionary heliplane, the V-22 Osprey, is reporting for duty.

... (on camera): The appeal of the V-22 is that it combines the best of both worlds. It can hover like a helicopter and fly like a plane.

... Wolf, I've got to tell you, after flying in this, if I was trapped in a hot landing zone, this is what I would want to come get me.

10 Consider the words of Colin Powell that "the only thing that can really destroy us is *us*." Here's the context of the quote: "You can drive up the road from here and come to a spot where there is a megachurch over here, a little Episcopal church over there, a Catholic church around the corner that's almost cathedral-size, and between them is a huge Hindu temple. There are no police needed to guard any of this. There are not many places in the world where you would see that. Yes, there are a few dangerous nuts in Brooklyn and New Jersey who want to blow up Kennedy Airport and Fort Dix. These are dangerous criminals, and we must deal with them. But come on, this is not a threat to our survival! The only thing that can really destroy us is *us*. We shouldn't do it to ourselves, and we shouldn't use fear for political purposes—scaring people to death so they will vote for you, or scaring people to death so that we create a terror-industrial complex" ("GQ Icon: Colin Powell," interview by Walter Isaacson, *GQ*, October 2007, http://men.style.com/gq/features/landing?id=content_5900).

11 *Ursprache* is a hypothetical parent language from which other languages derive. Some scholars, including German philosopher Walter Benjamin, believed there was a universal language that gives meaning to all speech. The root word *ur* has also been linked to the biblical Ur, home of the Tower of Babel, where languages were created.

12 For more on the emperor cult, see Richard A. Horsley, *Jesus and Empire: The Kingdom of God and the New World Disorder* (Minneapolis: Augsburg Fortress, 2003), esp. 22–24. For additional background see John Dominic Crossan, *God and Empire: Jesus Against Rome: Then and Now* (San Francisco: HarperOne, 2007), 23–25.

13 See, for example, the *Martyrdom of Polycarp*, a second-century account of the death of Polycarp, who was a disciple of John. At one point, Polycarp's persecutors ask, "What harm is there in saying, Caesar is Lord, and offering incense?" He refused and ultimately was killed for it (*Polycarp* 8:2, trans. J. B. Lightfoot).

14 "Mission Accomplished" speech delivered by President George W. Bush on May 1, 2003, aboard the USS *Abraham Lincoln*. He encouraged the troops that wherever the U.S. military goes, it carries "a message of hope 'to the captives, "Come out!" and to those in darkness, "Be free!"'" quoting Isaiah 49:9.

15 Genesis 4:10.

CHAPTER ONE **THE CRY OF THE OPPRESSED**

1 You can see the priority given to Exodus in the way the Jews were instructed to remember God. The Old Testament refers to God much more often as "the God who brought you out of Egypt" (thirty-two times) than it does to God as "Creator" (six times). The exodus event is the context in which the creation story is given. Creation and liberation are tied together because liberation of exiled creation is central to the story of the Bible. The center of gravity of the Jewish memory is, therefore, less the abstract account of creation than the concrete event of exodus. Martin Luther's translation of the Bible into German helps illustrate this point. His title for Genesis, "1 Moses" ("The First Book of Moses"), makes it clear that "in the beginning God created" was first spoken to liberated slaves through Moses. The Hebrew scholar John Durham (PhD from Oxford) argues this same point, beginning his commentary with the statement, "The Book of Exodus is the first book of the Bible" (John Durham, *Exodus*, Word Biblical Commentary, vol. 3 [Waco, TX: Word, 1987], xix).

The thirty-two references to "the God who brought you out of Egypt": Exodus 3:12; 6:7; 20:2; 29:46; 32:1; 32:4; 32:8; 32:11; 32:23; Leviticus 11:45; 19:36; 22:33; 25:38; 25:55; 26:13; 26:45; Numbers 15:41; Deuteronomy 5:6; 8:14; 13:5; 13:10; 20:1; Joshua 24:17; Judges 2:12; 6:8; 1 Kings 9:9; 12:28; 2 Kings 17:7; 2 Chronicles 7:22; Nehemiah 9:18; Psalm 81:10; Daniel 9:15.

The six references to "the Creator": Deuteronomy 32:6; Ecclesiastes 11:5; 12:1; Isaiah 27:11; 40:28; 43:15.

2   Exodus 1 and 5.

3   Exodus 3:7–9.

4   *The JPS Torah Commentary* calls *sa'aq* "one of the most powerful words in the [Hebrew] language. Pervaded by moral outrage and soul-stirring passion, it denotes the anguished cry of the oppressed, the agonized pleas of the helpless victim" (Nahum Sarna, *The JPS Torah Commentary: Exodus* [Philadelphia: Jewish Publication Society of America, 1991], 15). Walter Brueggemann calls the Exodus cry the "primal scream that permits the beginning of history." (How awesome is that?) He goes on to define *sa'aq*: "On the one hand it is a cry of misery and wretchedness with some self-pity, while it also functions for the official filing of a legal complaint. The mournful one is the plaintiff.... Israel does not voice resignation but instead expresses a militant sense of being wronged with the powerful expectation that it will be heard and answered" (Walter Brueggemann, *The Prophetic Imagination*, 2nd ed. [Minneapolis: Fortress, 2001], 11–12).

5   Genesis 4:24.

6   Joe Ehrman, the NFL defensive lineman turned preacher/social activist, used the term "anti-kingdom" in his teaching at Grace Fellowship Church in Timonium, Maryland. Don was a part of this community and heard Joe use this phrase on more than one occasion between 2001 and 2005.

7 Shalom includes "everything that constitutes healthy, harmonious life"; it is "the negation of lack" on every level. See Ernst Jenni and Claus Westermann, *The Theological Lexicon of the Old Testament*, vol. 3 (Peabody, MA: Hendrickson, 1997), 1337–48, particularly the bottom of 1343.

8 Exodus 5.

9 Genesis 11:3 says, "'Come, let's make bricks and bake them thoroughly.' They used brick instead of stone, and tar for mortar."

10 1 Corinthians 10:2.

11 Exodus 15, "The Song of Moses and Miriam," the first worship song in the Bible. "What may be the oldest piece of sustained poetry in the Hebrew Bible: a paean of praise to God, the biblical way of expressing gratitude" (Sarna, *JPS Torah Commentary*, 75).

12 Noah in Genesis 6 and Abraham in Genesis 12.

13 Exodus 19:15, 17.

14 According to *The JPS Torah Commentary*, "The idea of a covenantal relationship between God and an entire people is unparalleled" (Sarna, *JPS Torah Commentary*, 102). Abraham Joshua Heschel put it as only he could: "We have never been the same since the day on which the voice of God overwhelmed us at Sinai" (Abraham Joshua Heschel, *God in Search of Man: A Philosophy of Judaism* [New York: Farrar, Straus, and Giroux, 1955], 167).

15 Somebody somewhere pointed this out to us, and we don't remember where or when or who. If it was you, well done. Dinner is on us.

16 Exodus 19:4. Don heard the late David Mills preach a sermon on this passage in 1994 to a group of pastors in a small Russian village. The seminal idea of "church" that comes from this passage changed his life. It seems to have had a similar effect on the apostle Peter as well (1 Pet. 2:9).

17 Exodus 19:5.

18 "The origin of the Old Testament word has been debated; some have said it comes from a custom of eating together (Gen. 26:30; 31:54); others have emphasized the idea of cutting an animal," as in God's covenant with Abraham in Genesis 15:10–21 (Walter A. Elwell, *Evangelical Dictionary of Biblical Theology* [Grand Rapids: Baker, 1996], 124).

19 Exodus 19:5–6.

20 Exodus 7:1.

21 Exodus 19:6.

22 We've opted to use the word Israelite throughout this book instead of Hebrew. But the term Hebrew offers much to the narrative. Some scholars link the Hebrews to a nomadic people group called the Habiru, who settled in the ancient Near East in the second millennium BCE. There is scholarly debate about this linkage, but Walter Brueggemann is one of those scholars making such a link. If this is the case, he writes, "then the early references to what became of Israel are linked to a border social movement of marginal, precarious peoples. Recent scholarship has indicated that the term is not ethnic but sociological and refers to those at the edge of economic and political viability in many states in the region" (Brueggemann, *Prophetic Imagination*, 134 n. 4). He refers to the sociological work of Norman K. Gottwald, *The Tribes of Yahweh: A Sociology of the Religion of Liberated Israel, 1250–1050 BC* (Maryknoll, NY: Orbis, 1979).

23 Exodus 20:2.

24 This is called incarnation, from the Latin *incarnatio*, which means "taking on flesh" (*Eerdmans Bible Dictionary* [Grand Rapids: Eerdmans, 1987], 520).

25 Exodus 20:3.

26 Verse 4.

27 Verse 7.

28 The Hebrew *n's'*, "to carry" or "to take up" (Sarna, *JPS Torah Commentary*, 111).

29 Exodus 20:8.

30 The Sabbath command should be understood as being against the inhumane labor conditions and unreasonable production demands of Pharaoh's Egypt. The text says that "Pharaoh's slave drivers beat the Israelite overseers they had appointed, demanding, 'Why haven't you met your quota of bricks?'" (Exod. 5:14). How beautiful, then, is a God who commands these Israelites to rest each week?

31 Exodus 21–23.

32 Exodus 22:26–27.

33 Exodus 22:21–22; 23:6.

34 Exodus 22:23.

35 Exodus 19:5.

36 1 Kings 10.

37 1 Kings 10:9.

38 The Bible is full of stories in which the "pagan" characters seem to have better insight into the ways of God than the people who are supposed to have that insight. See Jethro in Exodus 18, Rahab in Joshua 2, the magi in the Gospels, and in Numbers 22 we're not sure about Balaam's donkey.

39 1 Kings 9:15. LORD spelled with all capitals, as it is in this verse, is an English attempt to honor the ancient, mysterious name of God, spelled YHVH. For more information, see Lawrence Kushner's *God Was in This Place, and I, I Did Not Know* (Woodstock, VT: Jewish Lights, 1993).

40 Exodus 19:4.

41 1 Kings 9:15.

42 See *Eerdmans Bible Dictionary*. "Solomon rebuilt and fortified the city [Hazor] as a garrison" (469) and Megiddo as "an administrative and military center" (706). Gezer was a bit different. 1 Kings 9:16 says that the pharaoh of Egypt at that time captured Gezer, set it on fire, killed its Canaanite inhabitants, and gave it as a wedding present to his daughter when she married Solomon. That extra-special something to get the newlyweds off to a good start.

43 1 Kings 10:26.

44 Verse 29.

45 1 Kings 11:3–4.

46 Deuteronomy 17:16–17.

47 1 Kings 10:14.

48 Assuming a prophet is simply someone who speaks for God, you could say that the queen of Sheba gets the whole prophetic thing started when she affirms the justice and righteousness intentions of God during her visit with Solomon. Not long after her visit, the prophet Ahijah announces Solomon's downfall (1 Kings 11), followed a few generations later by the prophet Jehu (1 Kings 16). Pretty soon you come to the prophets who were famous enough to get their own books in the Bible, names like Amos, Isaiah, and Micah. (Thanks to Ben Irwin for the language of this time line.)

49 Amos 3:1, 9–10.

50 Verse 15.

51 Isaiah 1:15.

52 Verses 13–14.

53 While there is no textual justification for using *church* here, there is a theological reason that we do so. Theologians from a variety of traditions have held that there has only ever been one people of God. Isaiah is bringing a message in this passage to God's people, Israel. Assemblies were the closest things they had to what we know as church.

54 Amos 4:1. Amos's "cows of Bashan" is a call back to a song in Deuteronomy 32:14. The TNIV titles it "The Song of Moses," but it could also be titled "The Song of the Second Exodus." It laments the punishment that will fall on Israel after she takes up the land, becomes fat off the choice cows of Bashan, and forgets God. Deuteronomy 32 is also a cry of hope for the mercy that will follow Israel's future exile, a hope that will influence the trajectory of the Bible and its pursuit of another deliverer to lead another exodus.

55 Amos 5:23; 8:4, 6.

56 Amos 6:7.

57 Amos 7:12–13.

58 Verses 14–17.

59 2 Chronicles 36:15.

60 Verse 16.

61 People are reluctant to ascribe human characteristics to God, such as suffering or searching, because it implies that God changes or is incomplete. But a God who suffers over the human condition and searches for a body to relieve that suffering is a critical aspect of Jewish theology. Abraham Joshua Heschel titles the whole of his philosophy of Judaism "God in Search of Man," claiming that "not only does man need God, God is also in need of man. It is such knowledge that makes the soul of Israel immune to despair" (Heschel, *God in Search of Man*, 196). Jewish theology seems quite prepared to accept a God who becomes man, while Christian theology embraces the belief that God already has.

62 2 Chronicles 36:17–20.

CHAPTER TWO **GET DOWN YOUR HARPS**

1 Psalm 137:1–4. See also the reggae song "Rivers of Babylon." (Thanks to anonymous theological reviewer #1, who corrected us. Bob Marley did not write "Rivers of Babylon." Brent Dowe and Trevor McNaughton did. It gives us great hope for the theological academy when its finest minds are also proficient in Jamaican popular music.)

2 Rob swears he heard Anne Lamott say this somewhere. If she did, then we want to make sure she gets proper credit. If she didn't, well, Rob is still available for lunch.

3 Isaiah 40:31. The verse says that "those who hope in the LORD will renew their strength. They will soar on wings like eagles; they will run and not grow weary, they will walk and not be faint." The inspirational language is easy to interpret in personal spirituality terms, but in its day it was one part political instigation, one part theological aspiration. Something like, "We've been down way too long, God's gonna come through, we're leaving Babylon, leaving exile, no one can stop us, we won't grow weary, God will swing low to rescue us from this place." And this verse comes from Isaiah 40, a central new exodus passage in Isaiah. We will see later in the Bible how important this passage is to the gospel writers.

4 Isaiah 11:11.

5 Isaiah 43:18–19.

6 Isaiah 66:18.

7 Isaiah 40:3.

8 Verse 5.

9 Isaiah 48:20.

10 Exodus 13:21; 23:20.

11 Exodus 19:5.

12 Deuteronomy 11:26; 30:1.

13 Exodus 32. The golden calf was a huge and tragic incident in the history of Israel. The Bible views the event at Sinai, the covenant between Israel and God, as a marriage contract. When Israel worships the golden calf, it's considered an act of unfaithfulness in marriage, or adultery. And the consequence for adultery, according to the law, was death (Deut. 22:22). Therefore, in the eyes of the law, Israel "died" to the marriage before the ink had even dried on the covenant. This national infidelity would continue to the point that the prophets came to view Israel as a prostitute (Hos. 9:1; Amos 7:17; Mic. 1:7).

14 Deuteronomy 30:1–10.

15 !

16 Isaiah 40:2.

17 Hosea 2:14. Hosea's "speak tenderly" is a commentary on Isaiah's "speak tenderly," which is a commentary on Moses's predictions in Deuteronomy 30:3 that God "will bring you back from captivity and have compassion on you and gather you again from all the nations where he scattered you."

18 Isaiah 54:5–6.

19 Isaiah 62:5.

20 Jeremiah 31:32.

21 See Exodus 20:19.

22 Jeremiah 31:33. This is a call back to Deuteronomy 30:2. In that passage Moses sees Israel's exile and eventual return. He says that it will be after this return that Israel will finally obey the covenant from the heart. Paul sees that day come to pass. Whereas Moses was depressed at Israel's behavior, saying, "If you have been rebellious against the LORD while I am still alive and with you, how much more will you rebel after I die!" (Deut. 31:27), Paul, on the other hand, is delighted by how the Philippians "have always obeyed—not only in my presence, but now much more in my absence" (Phil. 2:12). Paul celebrates the great reversal brought about by the new exodus that Moses and Jeremiah could only hope for.

23 Zechariah 8:3.

24 Isaiah 2:4.

25 Ezekiel 43:10.

26 Isaiah 66:20.

27 Isaiah 2:2.

28 Zechariah 2:4.

29 Isaiah 19:19–20.

30 Verse 21.

31 Verse 23a.

32 Verse 23b.

33 Verses 24–25.

34 The hatred with which the Jews held the Assyrians is nowhere more explicitly stated than in the last line of Psalm 137: "Happy are those who seize your infants and dash them against the rocks" (v. 9).

35 Isaiah 49:6; 52:10; 62:11.

36 Isaiah 65:17; 66:22.

37 Isaiah 65:25.

38 Isaiah 51:3.

39 Deuteronomy 18:15; see also Deuteronomy 30–32.

40 Isaiah 9:6–7.

41 1 Kings 10:9.

42 Isaiah 42.

43 Isaiah 61:1.

44 Isaiah 52:13.

45 1 Kings 3.

46 Jeremiah 23:5; 33:15.

47 Jeremiah 33:17. See also 1 Chronicles 22:10.

48 2 Samuel 7:16, emphasis added.

49 Ezekiel 37:25, emphasis added.

50 Genesis 3:15.

51 Isaiah 54:1.

CHAPTER THREE **DAVID'S OTHER SON**

1 Haggai 2:3.

2 Exodus 12:40–41.

3 See Nehemiah 13:6–7, which puts Nehemiah's final return to Jerusalem sometime after the "thirty-second year of Artaxerxes king of Babylon," which was in 433/432 BC. (A concise explanation can be found in the *TNIV Study Bible*, pages 721 and 735.)

4 Each gospel account includes Isaiah 40:3 at the beginning of the narrative. See Matthew 3:3; Mark 1:2–3; Luke 3:4–6; and John 1:23.

5 Matthew 15:22.

6 Mark 10:46–52.

7 Luke 18:39.

8 We keep using the phrase *suspended promises* because it is key to a New Exodus reading. The New Testament is understood as a Jewish book about Jewish promises fulfilled by a Jewish Messiah who comes to redeem all humanity from sin and death. This way of reading holds that what the New Testament was saying to its first hearers was wrapped up in the emotional and intellectual impact these suspended promises had on first-century Jews. In fact, you can't really understand Paul or the other writers of the New Testament unless you understand the emotional weight of these suspended promises. See Tom Holland, *Contours of Pauline Theology* (Ross-shire, Scotland: Christian Focus, 2004), 30.

9 John 2:1–12. Isaiah compares Israel's faithlessness to choice wine diluted by water (Isa. 1:22), but Jesus turns this curse on its head by turning water into choice wine—"but you have saved the best [wine] till now" (John 2:10). How awesome is that?

10 See Isaiah 25:6; 55:1. For Jeremiah, Israel was a bride turned cold from the love and devotion she once had for her husband (Jer. 2:1–2). God tells Hosea to marry a prostitute (Hos. 1:2) as a picture of what life with unfaithful Israel was like. But Isaiah saw a future wedding coming when God would marry a faithful bride. This wedding was central to the coming new exodus (Isa. 49:18; 61:10; 62:5), and it would be a time of such joy that the wine would flow even to the poor (Isa. 55:1). Isaiah says elsewhere that "the LORD Almighty will prepare a feast of rich food for all peoples, a banquet of aged wine—the best of meats and the finest of wines" (Isa. 25:6). For Jews clinging to these suspended promises, Jesus's first miracle—turning water into wine at a wedding—was performance art of the highest consequence.

11 Luke 9:31.

12 John 14:6, emphasis added.

13 See Isaiah 30:21; 35:8; 40:3; 48:17; 57:14; 62:10; among others.

14 See Luke 9:51, 53; 13:22; 17:11; 18:31; 19:28; among others.

15 John 4:21.

16 Matthew 12:6.

17 Ezekiel 43.

18 Mathew 6:10; Mark 9:1; 11:10.

19 Matthew 13:24, 52; 18:23; Mark 4:26.

20 Matthew 12:28.

21 Mathew 3:2; 4:17; 10:7; Mark 1:15; Luke 10:9.

22 See Matthew, Mark, Luke, and John.

23 Matthew 11:3.

24 Verses 4–6. See Isaiah 29:18–19; 35:5–6.

25 Isaiah 42.

26 See Matthew 3:16; Mark 1:10; and Luke 3:22.

27 Genesis 1:2. "Hovering" comes from the word *rahap* (*rhp*). "The action of an eagle hovering over its young before it flies off. *Rhp* is also found in Ugaritic to describe birds' flight" (Gordon J. Wenham, *Word Biblical Commentary: Genesis 1–15* [Waco, TX: Word, 1987], 17).

28 John 1:1.

29 Matthew 13:38; 24:14; 26:13; John 12:19.

30 Matthew 24:14; 25:32; 28:19; Mark 13:10; Luke 24:47.

31 Matthew 24:30; Luke 2:10; 3:6; 7:29; John 1:4; 12:32.

32 Matthew 11:27; 19:28; Mark 9:12; Luke 10:22; John 1:3; 13:3.

33 Luke 24:13–35.

34 Verse 18.

35 Verse 21.

36 Matthew 9:27–31.

37 Matthew 22:41–46.

38 See Matthew 12:17–18; 20:26; 23:11; Mark 9:35; 10:43; among others.

39 Luke 24:25a.

40 Verse 25b.

41 Verse 26.

42 Verse 27.

43 Walter Wink's *Engaging the Powers* (Minneapolis: Augsburg Fortress, 1992) is a very helpful book explaining the myth of redemptive violence.

44 Matthew 26:52.

45 Verse 54.

46 Isaiah 52:13–15.

47 Deuteronomy 28.

48 Assuming an average walking speed of 2 to 3 mph, it would take between two and three hours to walk the distance (approximately seven miles) between Jerusalem and Emmaus. Thanks again to Ben Irwin for the insight.

49 Luke 24:31–32.

CHAPTER FOUR **GENITAL-FREE AFRICANS**

1 Acts 8:26–40.

2 Acts 1:3.

3 Verse 8.

4 Isaiah 5:26; 24:16; 45:22; 48:20; 49:6.

5 Acts 8:34.

6 Acts 2:1.

7 See Midrash to Exodus (*Shemot Rabbah* 29).

8 See the School of Ishmael (*b. Shabbat* 88a). See also Abraham Joshua Heschel, Gordon Tucker, and Leonard Levin, *Heavenly Torah: As Refracted through the Generations* (New York: Continuum International Publishing Group, 2005), 252.

9 Acts 2:3.

10 Verse 5.

11 Verses 9–11.

12 Verse 13.

13 Exodus 32:28.

14 Acts 2:41.

15 Johannes Blauw offers an insightful summary of Genesis 1–11 in his book *The Missionary Nature of the Church* (New York: McGraw-Hill, 1962), 119.

16 1 Corinthians 10:2.

17 Acts 8:36.

18 Deuteronomy 23:1.

19 Thanks to Ben Irwin for pointing this out to us.

20 Acts 9:1–2, emphasis added.

21 God called the prophet Ezekiel and told him to "get up and go out to the plain," where God would speak to him (Ezek. 3:22). When Paul was called to serve God, he was told to get up and go to the desert of Arabia, where God would speak to him (Acts 9:6; Gal. 1:16–17). The point in these stories is that the commission given to both comes not from human origin but from God directly.

22 Acts 9:15.

23 Acts 15:1–2.

24 Galatians 5:12.

25 See Tom Holland's *Contours of Pauline Theology* (Ross-shire, Scotland: Christian Focus, 2004), 90.

26 See Romans 6:6. For more on the "body of sin," see Holland's *Contours of Pauline Theology*, 85–110.

27 Romans 7:24.

28 Paul clearly isn't against the practice of circumcision in its own right. In Acts 16 when Paul wanted to take Timothy along on his missionary journey, the text says that "he circumcised him because of the Jews who lived in that area, for they all knew that his father was a Greek" (v. 3). If you're Timothy, do you question this bit of theology? "Paul, seriously—you're sure about this?"

29 2 Corinthians 6:17.

30 2 Corinthians 5:17.

31 Galatians 6:15.

32 Acts 10.

33 Acts 10:28a.

34 Verse 28b.

35 Psalm 20:7.

36 Isaiah 2:4.

37 Acts 1:6.

38 There's an ancient tradition that says the queen of Sheba came from Ethiopia. How great would *that* be? It's all connected, isn't it?

39 Genesis 12.

40 Acts 8:1.

41 Acts 2:44–45.

42 Romans 15:26; 2 Corinthians 8:19; Galatians 2:10.

43 Isaiah 60:5, 11; 61:6; 66:12, 19–21.

44 Acts 8:39.

45 Exodus 19:23.

46 1 Chronicles 23:13.

47 Numbers 4:4–17.

48 Leviticus 20:26.

49 Acts 13:2.

50 Isaiah 61:6. The Christian doctrine of "the priesthood of all believers" is rooted in the redemption of Israel and their calling by God at Sinai as a "kingdom of priests" (Exod. 19:6).

51 Romans 15:16.

52 Acts 28:23a.

53 Verse 23b.

54 Verses 30–31.

CHAPTER FIVE **SWOLLEN-BELLIED BLACK BABIES, SOCCER MOMS ON PROZAC, AND THE MARK OF THE BEAST**

1 The story of Dora Farms and the quotes from Iraqi civilians and U.S. military representatives are taken from the documentary *Why We Fight* by Eugene Jarecki.

2 U.S. Secretary of Defense Donald Rumsfeld, U.S. Department of Defense news briefing, March 21, 2008.

3 Much has been said and written about empire, a lot of which is angry and cynical. There are some serious books, however, that deserve reading and reflection. From the historical perspective, Edward Gibbon's *The History of the Decline and Fall of the Roman Empire* (Penguin Classic abridged edition, 2001) is a classic that deserves attention. To engage the contemporary academic discussion, Michael Hardt and Antonio Negri's *Empire* (Cambridge, MA: Harvard University Press, 2000) is an important book, but you'll have to work for it. Theologically, much of the writing of Walter Brueggemann deals with the topic, especially its relation to the Old Testament. Brian Walsh and Sylvia Keesmaat's *Colossians Remixed* (Downers Grove, IL: InterVarsity, 2004) is simply a great work. The opening *targum* is outstanding.

4 According to *The CIA World Factbook*, world GDP (gross domestic product, a measure of economic power) was nearly $65 trillion in 2006. That same year, American GDP was a little over $13 trillion.

5 According to the International Database for the U.S. Census Bureau, estimated world population is just under 6.7 billion as of May 2008. Total U.S. population stands around 304 million.

6 UNICEF, *Progress for Children: A World Fit for Children Statistical Review* 6 (December 2007), 40. See also Bret Schulte, "A World of Thirst," *U.S. News and World Report*, May 27, 2007. Americans are the world's biggest users of water.

7 UNICEF, *Progress for Children*, 18, and UNICEF, *Biovision Children's Forum*, March 2007.

8 Timothy W. Jones, "Using Contemporary Archaeology and Applied Anthropology to Understand Food Loss in the American Food System" (Tucson, AZ: Bureau of Applied Research in Anthropology, University of Arizona, 2004).

9 World Bank, *World Development Indicators 2007*. See also United Nations, *The Millennium Development Goals Report 2007*, 6. It is important to note that "dollars per day" does not define what one U.S. dollar would purchase in a poor country, which might be quite a lot. "Dollars per day" is a creation of the World Bank to measure what is called "purchasing power parity" or PPP. PPP measures what things cost around the world, allowing for exchange rates. In short, to say that a woman in Burundi lives on one dollar per day is to say that she can buy in one day in her world what you can buy for one dollar in yours. For more on this, go to the Organisation for Economic Co-operation and Development website (www.oecd.org) and search on "PPP."

10 World Bank, *World Development Indicators 2007*.

11 Mintel Consumer, Media and Marketing Research, as cited in "Teen Spending Estimated to Top $190 Billion by 2006," Market Research Portal, November 12, 2004.

12 UNICEF, *Progress for Children*, 40.

13 "Solving the Diaper Dilemma," *Real Money*, January–February 2003.

14 United Nations Development Programme (UNDP), *Human Development Report 2007/2008*, 44.

15 UNESCO Institute for Statistics, "Estimates and Projections of Adult Illiteracy for Population Aged Fifteen Years and Above, by Country and by Gender, 1970–2015," July 2002.

16 UNICEF, *Progress for Children*, 12.

17 It is probably the case that more than 90 percent of the world does not own a car. See Richard Register, "Green Cities and the End of the Age of Oil," *Common Ground Magazine*, June 2005.

18 Experian Automotive, "New Study Shows Multiple Cars Are King in American Households," February 12, 2008.

19 UNICEF, *Progress for Children*, 45.

20 U.S. Census Bureau, "High School Graduation Rates Reach All-Time High; Non-Hispanic White and Black Graduates at Record Levels," June 29, 2004.

21 See Oliver James, *Affluenza* (London: Vermillion, 2007).

22 This remains true despite the United States's disappointing twelfth-place showing in the 2007 Human Development Index (http://hdr.undp.org/en/media/hdr_20072008_tables.pdf). Apparently, Iceland, Norway, Australia, Canada, Ireland, Sweden, Switzerland, Japan, the Netherlands, France, and Finland all enjoy a better standard of living than does America. As much as we like Sigur Rós, this does not change the dynamics of empire or the reality of American military, economic, and cultural influence around the globe. Neither do we suggest that this dominance is immune to the rise of other great powers or to our own economic uncertainties. If anything, the biblical story teaches us that no nation is entitled to global dominance, no matter how powerful their national myths may be.

23 Shankar Vedantam, "Antidepressant Use by U.S. Adults Soars," *Washington Post*, December 3, 2004.

24 Deuteronomy 8:12–14.

25 Exodus 22:22; Deuteronomy 10:18; 14:29; 16:11, 14; 24:17, 19–21; 26:12–13; 27:19; Job 24:3; Psalms 94:6; 146:9; Jeremiah 7:6; 22:3; Ezekiel 22:7; Zechariah 7:10; Malachi 3:5; James 1:27.

26 Deuteronomy 8:17–18.

27 Attributed to George H. W. Bush at the Rio Earth Summit in 1992.

There's some question as to whether Bush himself said this or his delegates. *Time* magazine reported that "while senior officials held briefings painting the Bush Administration as pro-environment, U.S. delegates backed the status quo on one topic after another, insisting over and over that 'the American life-style is not up for negotiation'" (Philip Elmer-Dewitt, "Summit to Save the Earth: Rich vs. Poor," *Time*, June 1, 1992).

28 All oil statistics listed can be verified by two web-based sources. The first is the Energy Information Administration website, which is the official energy statistics provider of the U.S. government (http://tonto.eia.doe.gov/country/index.cfm). The second, Gibson Consulting (http://www.gravmag.com/oil.html#consume), parses the data from EIA. Note the EIA country lists for leading consumption, production, importing, and exporting countries (http://tonto .eia.doe.gov/country/index.cfm#countrylist), which is easy to access, and the Reference Case Projections, Table A4, "World Oil Consumption by Region, Reference Case 1990–2030," for percentage of global oil consumption (http://www.eia.doe.gov/oiaf/ ieo/pdf/ieoreftab_4.pdf). The illustration of what twenty million barrels per day looks like is provided by Gibson Consulting, based on forty-two-gallon barrels.

29 General Anthony Zinni's testimony to the Senate Armed Services Committee, April 13, 1999, cited by James A. Paul in "Iraq: The Struggle for Oil," Global Policy Forum website, December 2002, http://www.globalpolicy.org/security/oil/2002/08jim.htm.

30 George Washington, in his farewell address on September 17, 1796, instructed his successors to "avoid the necessity of those overgrown military establishments, which, under any form of government, are inauspicious to liberty, and which are to be regarded as particularly hostile to Republican Liberty." One hundred sixty-five years later, Republican president and war hero Dwight D. Eisenhower saw America's huge military and the large private arms industry attached to it as unprecedented threats to the American experience. His warning is stern: "In the councils of government, we must guard against the acquisition of unwarranted influence, whether sought or unsought, by the military-industrial complex. The potential for the disastrous rise of misplaced power exists and will persist. We must never let the weight of this combination endanger our liberties or democratic processes. We should take nothing for granted. Only an alert and knowledgeable citizenry can compel the proper meshing of the huge industrial and military machinery of defense with our peaceful methods and goals, so that security and liberty may prosper together" (farewell address, January 17, 1961).

31 The Center for Arms Control and Non-Proliferation, "The FY 2009 Pentagon Spending Request—Global Military Spending," February 22, 2008.

32 "World Wide Military Expenditures," www.globalsecurity.org.

33 See "Budget of the United States Government, Fiscal Year 2009," Office of Management and Budget, www.whitehouse.gov/omb/budget/fy2009. According to the summary tables, defense spending accounted for 51 percent of discretionary spending in the 2008 budget. In the budget proposed for fiscal year 2009, it will increase to 52 percent.

34 For an introduction to Native American culture and spirituality, we recommend John G. Neihardt's *Black Elk Speaks* (Lincoln: University of Nebraska Press, 1932).

35 Nuclear bombs were dropped on Hiroshima and Nagasaki on August 6, 1945, and August 9, 1945, respectively. "Two days later … the Japanese government sent an offer of surrender, with one condition: that the status of Japan's emperor be guaranteed. The next day, the Allies agreed to alter the terms of unconditional surrender…. On August 14, Radio Tokyo announced the government's acceptance of this clarification and, therewith, its surrender.

The war was over—and within weeks, journalists and historians began to debate whether it might have ended on similar terms and around the same time without the bomb" (Kai Bird and Martin J. Sherwin, *American Prometheus: The Triumph and Tragedy of J. Robert Oppenheimer* [New York: Knopf, 2005], 318).

Edward T. Linenthal's study of the controversy attempts to place it in context. "In the spring and summer of 1945 ... the American press engaged in lively debate over alternatives to unconditional Japanese surrender. There was vigorous disagreement among Manhattan Project scientists who made the atomic bomb about the wisdom of the decision to use it, and after the war's end, there was strong criticism of its use from many prominent Protestant and Catholic spokespeople." Linenthal cites William F. Buckley's conservative *National Review* in a May 1958 article that stated, "The tens of thousands of Japanese who were roasted at Hiroshima and Nagasaki were sacrificed not to end the war or save American and Japanese lives but to strengthen American diplomacy vis-à-vis Russia" (Edward T. Linenthal and Tom Engelhardt, eds., *History Wars* [New York: Holt, 1996], 10–11).

A surprising voice speaking against the necessity of the bomb was Dwight Eisenhower: "I voiced ... my grave misgivings, first on the basis of my belief that Japan was already defeated and that dropping the bomb was completely unnecessary, and secondly because I thought that our country should avoid shocking world opinion by the use of a weapon whose employment was, I thought, no longer mandatory as a measure to save American lives" (Dwight D. Eisenhower, *Mandate for Change: 1953–1956* [Garden City, NY: Doubleday, 1963], 312–13). Similar Eisenhower misgivings are recounted by his family members in the Eugene Jarecki documentary *Why We Fight*.

36 1 Kings 10:14; see also Revelation 13:18.

37 Isaiah 1:8.

38 See Exodus 6:9; Leviticus 26:27; Deuteronomy 1:43; Judges 2:17; 2 Kings 17:14; 2 Chronicles 36:15–16; Nehemiah 9:17; Psalm 81:11; Isaiah 28:12; 65:12; Jeremiah 6:17; 7:24; 11:8; 17:23; 25:4; 29:19; Ezekiel 3:7; Zechariah 1:4; 7:13.

39 Among the many commentaries on Revelation, we recommend Michael Wilcock's *Message of Revelation: I Saw Heaven Opened*, The Bible Speaks Today series (Downers Grove, IL: InterVarsity, 1975), and G. K. Beale's *The Book of Revelation: A Commentary on the Greek Text*, New International Greek Testament Commentary (Grand Rapids: Eerdmans, 1999).

40 Ethelbert Stauffer, *Christ and the Caesars* (London: SCM, 1955). For a stunning visual journey through the world of first-century Ephesus, see Ray Vander Laan's video series on Asia Minor, available through That the World May Know ministries (www.followtherabbi .com).

41 For more on emperor worship, the persecution of the church, and the context of the period, see Beale's *Book of Revelation*, esp. 4–33.

42 Revelation 13:16; 14:9; 16:2; 19:20; 20:4. See John Dominic Crossan's *God and Empire* (San Francisco: HarperOne, 2007) and Shane Claiborne and Chris Haw's *Jesus for President* (Grand Rapids: Zondervan, 2008).

43 See Luke 4:18.

CHAPTER SIX **BLOOD ON THE DOORPOSTS OF THE UNIVERSE**

1 Exodus 12.

2 Exodus 12:3, 8, 11.

3 Verses 12–13.

4 Exodus 4:22.

5 Exodus 12:26–27.

6 Isaiah 53.

7 Luke 2:4, 7. Scholars debate whether Matthew also uses the term firstborn in his account. The word *firstborn* (*prototokos* in Greek) is found in Matthew 1:25 in some Greek manuscripts, but not in others. Where it does appear, the verse says that Mary was a virgin until she gave birth to her firstborn. Because that seems redundant (could a virgin already have a child?), the NIV, TNIV, and NASB, following modern interpretive methods, leave out the word "firstborn" of Matthew 1:25. But textual critics and even early Greek scribes may have missed a very Jewish point. The urgency of Jewish hopes centered on God's firstborn as his chosen agent of a new and final exodus. Matthew's Jewish audience would have understood the implications of his redundant emphasis on God's firstborn. But give it up for good King Jimmy, for verily doth the KJV include "firstborn" in Matthew 1:25.

8 John 1:29.

9 Matthew 26:26–28; Mark 14:22–24; Luke 22:19–20.

10 Colossians 1:15. The "firstborn over all creation" has traditionally been understood as a reference to Proverbs 8 and the role of Wisdom in the creation event. But Tom Holland argues persuasively that this passage should be understood as a reference to the new exodus expectations of the first-century Jews. As we have learned, the Jewish people clung to the suspended promises related to another liberator. They understood what the firstborn had signified in the first exodus; his redemption meant the salvation of the Jewish household. Paul proclaimed in the Colossians hymn (Col. 1:15ff.)

that the victory Christ brought about by his blood far exceeded the old covenant and the first exodus. This is Paul's declaration of total redemption, liberation of the entire created order (Tom Holland, *Contours of Pauline Theology* [Ross-shire, Scotland: Christian Focus, 2004], 275–91).

11 See Colossians 1:20.

12 2 Corinthians 4:8–9.

13 Verse 10.

14 Verse 11.

15 Verse 12.

16 1 Corinthians 9:20–22.

17 2 Corinthians 11:29.

18 Ephesians 2:14–15a.

19 Verses 15b–16.

20 Acts 8:19.

21 Hebrews 10:24.

22 Though the anonymous writer of this book was writing in Greek, she was no doubt influenced by the Hebrew word (which shouldn't be surprising in a book called "Hebrews").

23 See 2 Corinthians 10:4.

24 Leviticus 19:9–10, 36.

25 Ephesians 3:10; see also 6:12.

26 Attributed to Archbishop William Temple and a favorite quote of the one and only Dr. Clive Calver.

27 Hebrew 12:24.

28 Genesis 4:10.

29 Colossians 1:13–14.

EPILOGUE **BROKEN AND POURED**

1 Kevin Bales, *Disposable People: New Slavery in the Global Economy* (Berkeley: University of California Press, 1999). See also Susan Llewelyn Leach, "Slavery Is Not Dead, Just Less Recognizable," *Christian Science Monitor*, September 1, 2004.

2 UNICEF, *State of the World's Children*, 2007; World Food Programme, *Counting the Hungry*, 2007.

3 World Health Organization. See also Shanoi Bhattacharya, "Global Suicide Toll Exceeds War and Murder," *NewScientist.com*, September 8, 2004.

4 UNAIDS, *AIDS Epidemic Update*, 2007. In 2007 there were 2.1 million AIDS-related deaths globally—approximately 5,700 each day. In Africa alone, 1.6 million people died because of AIDS—that's about 4,400 Africans each day.

5 Genesis 4:10.

6 Proverbs 10:15; 18:11.

7 Luke 16:19–31.

8 Exodus 3:10.

9 Revelation 21:4.

10 Luke 22:19.

DISCUSSION GUIDE

1   Rob Bell and Don Golden highlight a pattern at the heart of salvation history that plays out in four key places in the Bible: Egypt, Sinai, Jerusalem and Babylon. These four parts represent a cycle in which first, Christians have cried out to God (Egypt); then God has answered and delivered them, decreeing a new era of life (Sinai); followed by entering a time of blessedness, prosperity, and ultimately decline (Jerusalem); and finally experiencing a period of decline likened to exile (Babylon). How does this framework help you understand the spiritual journey taken by individuals as well as by churches? Do you recognize it as something you've seen before? How does it help us read and understand Jesus's story, and how do the priorities of Jesus inform our understanding of what it means to follow him today?

2   "Egypt," being "the superpower of its day" (p. 13), "is what happens when sin becomes structured and embedded in society" (p. 18). What, if anything, might

be considered a modern-day Egypt? Where is the church's place in it?

3 At Sinai, God speaks. "Before God speaks directly to the people, God tells Moses to remind them of the exodus [out of Egypt]. 'You yourselves have seen what I did to Egypt, and how I carried you on eagles' wings and brought you to myself.' It's all grace. It's all a gift" (pp. 21–22). Is there a contemporary equivalent to this kind of deliverance? What is the relationship between the gift of grace and the conditions in receiving it?

4 In Jerusalem, Solomon set up his throne and began his reign of power, prosperity, and righteousness. However, Solomon's story takes a tragic turn. What implications does this tragic story carry for Christians living in today's world generally, and in the United States specifically? Is it applicable only on a national level? Or can a church community also follow Solomon's path?

5 The final piece is Babylon, exile. The authors give a few definitions for what a person's life in exile might look like: "when you forget your story"; "when you fail to convert your blessings into blessings for others"; or "when you find yourself a stranger to the purposes of God" (p. 38). How might these versions of "exile" show themselves in the church today? Do any of the definitions apply to you personally or to your faith community? What concrete steps can a community take to "return from exile"?

6 Citing the prophet Isaiah, the authors write about a new plan, or new hope, that intervenes to stop the vicious cycle. What is the church's role in executing God's new plan? How do you see yourself as part of that effort?

7 Chapter 5 seems a strong indictment of American prosperity and its implications for the church. Do you think prosperity is a problem? Does it pose an issue for us spiritually? What burden, if any, does this disproportion of the world's wealth and resources impose on the American church?

8 In chapter 6 the authors assert that Christians are to assume the role of "the Eucharist" in the community of faith. "That's how the Eucharist works. For someone to receive, someone has to give" (p. 148). Had you understood the Eucharist in this way prior to reading this? Does this suggest that God's saving work is more communal than individually oriented? How can your faith community be a Eucharist for others?

9 Does the experience of Christians today parallel the journey of the ancient Israelites? What is the "Egypt" from which their cries arise? What might be the modern equivalent to "Sinai" where God presents promises? What is the "Jerusalem" to which God calls Christians? How might it come to pass that the believing community might find itself in a new "Babylon," in exile? (pp. 171–173). Have you seen examples of these in your own life or faith community? If so, share an experience. What cries does God hear today?

10 When the authors assert that Jesus wants to save Christians from a narrow view of the gospel (pp. 178–179), what is Jesus saving Christians *to?* What would a church that is "saved" look like? (pp. 179–180). Or, do you even think Christians and the church need to be saved?

11 How has *Jesus Wants to Save Christians* affected your understanding of the church's place in society? Has it changed your idea of individual responsibility and faithfulness in the context of a faith community? Are there any actionable steps that can be taken from this book and put into practice in your spiritual journey and/or the journey of your church?

ROB BELL is a bestselling author and international teacher and speaker whose books have captivated a new generation of Christians. Author of the bestselling books *Love Wins, Velvet Elvis, Sex God,* and *Drops Like Stars,* he also appeared in a pioneering series of short films called NOOMA. Bell was profiled in *Time* magazine as one of the 100 most influential people in the world in 2011. He and his wife, Kristen, have three children. Visit the author online at www.robbell.com.

DON GOLDEN is a church activist and vice president with World Relief in Baltimore, Maryland.

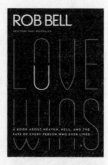